WHY WE HATE BLACK WOMEN

AND WHY WE SHOULD LOVE THEM

Blue Magic Publishing
Williamstown, NJ

Why We Hate Black Women
And Why We Should Love Them

Copyright 2010 © by Hasani Pettiford.
All rights reserved.
Published by Blue Magic Publishing, Inc., Williamstown, New Jersey.
Book edited by: Sological Underpennings
For general information on our other products and services or for technical support, please contact our Customer Care Department at 888-237-6101 (toll-free/fax).
Pettiford, Hasani.
Why We Hate Black Women / Hasani Petiford.
ISBN 978-0-9707915-6-6
Library of Congress Control Number: 2009913672

Dedication

I dedicate this book to the six most important women in my life. You all have made an impact on my life and I pray that this book will make an impact on yours. My mother has taught me character and invaluable life lessons that have helped to make me the man that I am. My wife has been my support and co-pilot throughout our entire relationship. After 7 years of marriage, I am still in love. My daughters and niece were my motivation for writing this book. My prayer is that it will impart both wisdom and instruction at an early age which will help them experience the life that they all deserve.

Danielle Pettiford
Paris Pettiford
Madison Pettiford
Savannah Pettiford
Shirley Pettiford
Tania Pettiford

About The Author

As an award-winning author and speaker, Hasani Pettiford has an appeal that transcends barriers of age, culture and occupation. For almost a decade Mr. Pettiford has been a recognized authority on human sexuality, interpersonal relationships and personal growth and development. Hasani has directly impacted the lives of many nationwide with his best-selling books and speaking engagements. Much of Pettiford's work has been featured in major

Hasani Pettiford

media outlets, including national publications, television and radio programs.

Hasani Pettiford is the founder of Hasani Pettiford Enterprises which is headquartered in New Jersey. His company offers public seminars, customized educational programs and materials and keynote addresses. Hasani has spoken for more than 1,000 audiences throughout the US and Africa. Hasani has a client list that includes fortune 500 companies, trade and civic associations, churches as well as colleges and universities.

Hasani is also a relationship coach who provides sound advice for singles and couples. Pettiford's work has been feature on theTBN, BET, TV-One, Black Enterprise Magazine and Gospel Today Magazine and many other media outlets. Hasani is happily married and has three children. He is active in the community and faith based affairs.

CONTENTS

Dedications
About the Author
Acknowledgements
Forward
Introduction: Why I Wrote This Book

Bonus Chapter: Black Women Who Want More
Notes
Appendix

Acknowledgement

This book could not have been written without the wisdom and support of my BEAUTIFUL BLACK WIFE Danielle Pettiford. Danielle serves as my graphic designer, book cover designer, web master, book publisher and most importantly supportive wife and mother of my children. Others who have contributed greatly to the content, editing and over intellectual substance of the book are as follows: T. Je'Nein Ferrell, Erica Lewis, Rachel Renee Griggs, Anecia Washington, Kim Marasco, Cheryl Addison, Michael D. Teague, my entire Facebook group, and everyone else who has offered a suggestion or word of encouragement about this project. Finally, I want to thank Renee Toppin and the entire Black Women Who Want More organization for all of your assistance with this project and future documentary. Thank you.

Forward

Black Women Who Want More approves this book. We are an organization of Black women who are striving to be spiritually grounded, emotionally stable, physically fit, financially poised, intellectually enlightened, politically conscious and socially gracious. We are women who want more, demand more and deserve more of the best that life has to offer.

The majority of Black women today are broken. There is some area of brokenness in our lives that causes us to manifest the behaviors that make us objects of the hatred that is spoken of in this book. Bitterness, nasty attitudes, and unrealistic expectations are products of the pain we feel when we brush across the cracks in our spirits.

Black Women Who Want More are on a journey to retrieve those fragmented pieces and restore wholeness. We are on a journey to become our best selves. As broken vessels, we must first consult the master builder, the potter who carefully crafted us and made us the beautiful creatures that we are. Spiritual wholeness is the first step in the journey. We must learn the art of submission; we must regain trust in God and reassert our trust in our Black men.

Once we are spiritually whole, the rest of the pieces will come together as our ordered steps take us forward in this journey. As we love ourselves MORE, others will love us MORE. As we respect ourselves MORE, others will respect us MORE. The hate will dissipate as we are seen in the light of our wholeness. We will be complete, no longer looking for someone else to complete us or to fill the empty spaces in our hearts, our bodies, our finances or our souls. This is the end of that journey, and the beginning of MORE.

Why We Hate Black Women is simply a book about broken women. Broken women have jagged edges. Broken women cut with their tongues and wound with their words. Broken women cut Black men, cut each other and cut themselves. Our relationships are covered with the blood of our brokenness.

We must acknowledge that our materialism, our inadequate self-respect, and our insufficient regard for other Black women, reflect scars that we must not allow to fester. We must cultivate the humility to listen to others as they describe their perceptions of us. We must change and we must heal: only then will we get MORE.

Why We Hate Black Women is designed to promote healing for a generation of women and the Black Family. There is a bruise on the image of Black Women in America and sadly we participate in our own injury. We have to regain our self-respect, recognize our beauty, and present a new image, which reflects our healing, to our men and to society.

When a woman is whole, she is empowered with a thoughtful confidence that is reflected in every area of her life. Just as a whole woman is careful and wise concerning her spiritual and mental well-being, she makes better decisions with regards to relationships, friendships, marriage, finances, and health. This wholeness allows her to expect and demand MORE out of life.

Renee Toppin
Black Women Who Want More
Founder, President

Why I Wrote This Book

Let me first start by saying that I LOVE BLACK WOMEN. My mother is Black. My sister is Black My wife is Black. My three daughters are Black. I am surrounded by beautiful, intelligent, spiritually strong Black women. So this is not about expressing why I hate Black women. I wrote this book because I am very concerned about the state of our women in this society. My children were the motivation for writing this book. As a father of three Black girls, I had to ask myself some very serious questions:

Where will my daughters be in 15 to 20 years? Will they be successful, single and undesirable? Will they be victims of sexual abuse or domestic violence? Will they be full of anger, bitterness, and pain due to past relationships? Will they be single mothers struggling to raise a family all by themselves? Will they have adversarial relationships with other Black women? Will they manifest an unconscious state of self-hatred? Will they have to constantly disprove the media-induced stereotypes that pigeonhole Black women? Will they be considered double minorities in a society that doesn't value their existence? As long as I am alive, my desire as a father will be to ensure that none of this happens.

Sadly, too many Black women experience the very things that I question regarding the future of my own daughters. As a Black man, I have mixed emotions concerning the current state of our women. I am happy for all of the successes and accomplishments of Black women. They have done so much and come so far in a society that has attempted to hold them back for so long. They are providers, protectors, nurturers, care-givers, leaders, entrepreneurs and so much more. But with those accomplishments has come a heavy price.

Why We Hate Black Women discusses a multitude of issues concerning Black women that need to be further discussed. This book does not address every historical, social, political, relational and personal issue concerning women. There aren't enough pages in this book to accomplish that. This book does not deal with every aspect of Black womanhood. No book does, so don't look for that. This book is not about why Black men hate Black women. It's much deeper than that.

This book discusses why we all have been socialized to hate Black women. The 'We' in Why We Hate Black Women consists of all races of people, the media, Hip Hop culture and much more. As this book reveals, we have all contributed towards the hatred of Black women

This book was written to do one primary thing: Challenge Black men and women to take an introspective look at ourselves in order to close the ever-increasing historical wedge in Black relationships, rebuild our families and restore our communities. This book will challenge all of us. It will challenge our thinking, our behavior, our identity and the harmful things that we've held on to for so long. Note: Additional chapters and the group study guide can be downloaded for free on the website http://www.whywehateblackwomen.com/

Black Women Are Valued By No One...

She had nothing to fall back on; not maleness, not whiteness, not ladyhood, not anything. And out of the profound desolation of her reality she may well have invented herself.
~Toni Morrison

*U*huru violently awoke in a Philadelphia hospital bed to the smell of gunpowder everywhere. After nine days of nightmares, flashbacks, strange noises in the middle of the night and throbbing pain that rippled through her body, finality quickly reared its ugly head. As she painfully reached over the hospital bedrail to grab the local paper placed on the night stand next to her, she read the front page headline that brought closure to yet another chapter in her life. Her high school sweetheart of 12 years was dead. Upon completion of the article somehow she knew this day would come.

As she calmly placed her head on her pillow, Uhuru began to journey back to the beginning of their relationship. It all began during her freshman year. Like most relationships they shared a lot of good times together. But as time passed, it became seasoned with great disappointment. From high school to college to careers, their eight year journey took them through many changes. They were no longer kids but young adults in a mature relationship which put a strain on their intimate connection.

Her hard work and educational accomplishments landed her a career as a nurse which led to the money, the house, and a number of other luxuries that he did not experience. Darin, on the other hand, worked for UPS. As Uhuru moved up the socioeconomic latter, Darin remained stuck and stagnant. Ultimately, feelings of jealousy and inadequacy loomed within Darin's heart and soul. Not only did his unresolved issues affect his relationship but his job as well.

Relationally, the atmosphere quickly became turbulent. Arguments, fights, habitual unfaithfulness, the exchange of STD's, multiple pregnancies and abortions, repetitive break-ups and relationship reruns set the tone for their co-existence. Meanwhile, his working environment began to take a turn for the worst.

Darin began having confrontations and physical altercations with fellow employees. He even threatened to kill his new supervisor and then take his own life. This, no doubt, led to his immediate termination. Hopping from job to job, facing financial hardships and dealing with the lost of both his aunt and grandmother led him into a depression. It was at that moment that he told Uhuru, "I wasn't meant to be on this earth. I won't make it past the age of 25. I want to drive myself off a bridge."

Darin's struggle with his internal demons set the stage for what would soon take place within their relationship. Their daily interaction became marred with verbal and physical abuse. His brown belt in martial arts became the weapon repeatedly used against Uhuru. With brute force he hit her at will. He would often grab her, twist her arm, throw her to the ground, slap her in the face and choke her while violently screaming profanities into the atmosphere. After numerous episodes of physical abuse Uhuru stopped fighting back.

Even during sexual union his aggressiveness made her feel as if she was being raped. He would choke her, push and hold her down, and hit her. Gripped by fear, she would lay there and take it. His behavior caused her to feel imprisoned in his presence. She wanted out but chose to stay because she felt like he needed her help. You see, Darin came from a family with mental health issues and he personally exhibited a mild case of schizophrenia, depression and attention deficit syndrome. So, in an attempt to protect him and his image, she hid her bruises and never told another living soul. Unbeknownst to her, the decision to stay soon became hazardous to her health.

On Thanksgiving Day Darin convinced Uhuru to join his family for dinner. As usual, he picked her up on the way to his parent's home but took an unexpected detour back to his apartment. After he convinced Uhuru to come inside, he locked her in with no foreseeable way out. Uncertain of his intentions, she quickly began to panic. With a sinister look in his eyes he pulled out his penis, pushed her to the floor and aggressively pulled her pantyhose down beneath her ankles. "I don't want to have sex", Uhuru screamed. Darin boisterously responded, "If you don't stay down, I'll get my gun."

With no way out, Uhuru began to cry as he ejaculated inside of her. Once the deed was done she demanded that he take her home. Three hours later she got a call from Darin telling her to go get checked out because he had unprotected sex with a prostitute two weeks ago. The call drove her into a panic for fear that she might have AIDS. Their next encounter resulted in a drag out fight between the both of them. Unfortunately, Uhuru left with a bloody nose, a bruised leg and a broken finger.

After this incident she finally mustered up enough courage to end the relationship. It was finally over. However, several weeks later, Darin began stalking her by showing up to her job, appearing at her bus stop and following her home.

One day he pulled up to her bus stop and told her to get in the car. She frantically said "No!" He responded, "If you don't get in the car you'll really see how crazy I am." She immediately ran off.

Several minutes later Darin caught up to her and wrestled her down in the middle of the street. Somehow she escaped and risked her life by running across an eight lane highway just to get away from him.

Why We Hate Black Women

Uhuru immediately called the police and filed a three year restraining order against him. After two months of absolutely no communication the phone rings. It's Darin. He wants her back. Once Uhuru says no he immediately hangs up the phone. One hour later, as she walks to the bus stop, she sees him walking towards her, talking to himself, and waving a gun in his hand.

Once they make eye contact Uhuru runs for help towards a woman she sees from a distance. But Darin was driven by his ruthless mission and he easily over took her. Upon capturing her, Darin maliciously grabs her by the throat. He then cocks his gun as shell casings fly into the air. With all the breath left in her body, she screams to the top of her lungs, "Somebody please help me, he's trying to kill me!"

They begin to wrestle to the ground. While struggling to protect herself, she grabs her cell phone and attempts to call 911. He forcefully knocks the phone out of her hand and grabs her by the neck while pressing the gun into her face. As he continues to assault her an unmarked car closes in on them. Suddenly, a voice of urgency shouts out, "Philly Police...put your gun down." As the officer pulls out his gun, he and Darin begin to argue back and forth.

Once Uhuru realizes that help has arrived, she gains a moment of safety and security. Lost in the moment, she shouts, "Why don't you just shoot me...go ahead, pull the trigger...shoot me...shoot me." In response, Darin pulls the trigger. However, the gun was aimed at the cop in the car. Though Darin stood two feet from the vehicle, he misses. The car immediate pulls off and calls for back-up.

Meanwhile, Uhuru continues to provoke him with the screams of "just shoot me, just shoot me!" With her left arm twisted and pinned to the ground, he aims the gun at the top of her arm and pulls the trigger. Uhuru is shot. Her limb begins to vibrate as pain travels up and down her left arm. No sooner than Uhuru could say "Oh my God, I've been shot, bullet two is forcefully wedged inside her abdomen.

14

Chapter 1: *Black Women Are Valued By No One*

As she clutches her stomach, Darin fires the next shot. Bullet three pierces her right side. While Uhuru rolls on the ground in excruciating pain, a sequence of bullets are released from the gun's chamber. With the gun now aimed at her face, Uhuru quickly turns her head as bullet four grazes her nose. Within seconds three more bullets tear through her body. One penetrates her right hip, another pierces her left hip, and the final bullet tears through her buttocks.

Darin had emptied the entire case of bullets on Uhuru in an effort to end her life. Although her body was riddled with bullets, her will to live wouldn't allow her to give up. With the sounds of sirens and helicopters swooping over a crowd of shocked onlookers, Uhuru heard a heavenly voice that said "It's okay, you can get up now." With all the strength she could muster, Uhuru rose from an enormous puddle of blood.

As she ran for cover she saw her ex boyfriend reloading his gun. Within seconds more shots rang out. Finally, upon the arrival of the police, a foot chase ensued. An eight-man police unit ran towards Darin from every direction leaving him with few options. Cornered with no place to escape, Darin shoved the gun into his mouth and pulled the trigger. Darin killed himself. Unaware of what had happened, Uhuru was hauled away in an ambulance.

During her grueling nine day hospital stay, Uhuru's body remained at the mercy of her physicians. Those seven bullets almost ended her life. After hours of intense surgery, sections of her stomach, appendix and small intestines were removed. Once released, she endured 2 months of physical healing, 9 months of psychiatric treatment and an indefinite diagnosis of PTSD (Post Traumatic Stress Disorder).

Uhuru is a Swahili word which means 'Freedom.' But for the last twelve years Uhuru was imprisoned within her own relationship. Though she was not constrained with physical chains, she was ensnared with issues of the heart. It's amazing the things we will both do and endure in the name of love.

Why We Hate Black Women

I often find it humorous that no matter where I travel everyone claims to love Black women, especially Black men. Whether I am speaking on a college campus, sitting in a television studio or being interviewed on the radio, Black men, in particular, adamantly say "I don't hate Black women! I love Black women!" First, I find it amusing that everyone automatically assumes that I'm exclusively talking about Black men in the title of the book. Second, if Black women are so undeniably loved and adored, why don't the facts bear it out?

If Black women as a group are loved, why are so many Black women alone? Why have they been abused, abandoned, betrayed, lied to, cheated on, devalued and hated for over 390 years? Why is it that 42.3 percent of Black women have never been married in comparison to 23 percent of White women? Why are over 70 percent of all Black households in this country run by single-parent mothers?

Why is homicide at the hands of a current or former intimate partner the number one killer of African-American women ages 15 to 34 (*Africana Voices Against Violence*, Tufts University, Statistics)? Why are Black women 15 times more likely than White women to be infected with the H.I.V. virus (Center For Disease Control)? Why are Black women the most un-partnered group in America and perhaps the world? Where's all the love?

Behind all of these statistics are the stories, like Uhuru's, of painful experiences Black women have endured over the centuries at the hands of men. But, the onslaught of hate doesn't begin and end with Black men. It extends well beyond intimate relationships. It is a hatred shared by many and expressed in a multitude of ways.

The Hatred of Black Women

The Penguin Dictionary of Psychology defines hate as a 'deep, enduring, intense emotion expressing animosity, anger, and hostility towards a person, group, or object'. Because hatred is believed to be long-lasting, it is considered to be more of an attitude or disposition than a temporary emotional state. It's an attitude that is often expressed with measurements of hostility, animosity, disgust, malice and demeaning treatment.

The sad part about this disposition of hatred is that while some are aware of how it is reflected in their words, deeds, and actions others are completely oblivious. Just think about it. By definition hate speech is speech attacking or disparaging a group or members of a group. Usually we think of hate speech in terms of race or sexual orientation. However, it can apply to any social group, even women. So, in Hip Hop culture, when artists refer to women as b-tches, hoochies, chicken heads, gold diggers, ho's, tricks and skeezas, it can be considered a form of hate speech. When a person's tongue is used as a weapon to verbally abuse a woman, thus shattering her self esteem, it's a form of hate speech.

What about hate crimes? Hate crimes refer to a criminal act towards a certain social group which may involve physical assault, verbal abuse, insults and a host of other oppressive behaviors. Can Black women qualify as one of these social groups? Sure they can. Just consider this story.

On June 18, 2007, a Black woman was gang raped by 10 youths (known as the Dunbar Village Rapists) and forced at gunpoint to have sex with her own 12 year old son in a housing complex called Dunbar Village in West Palm Beach, Florida. The young men not only viciously punched, kicked and sliced this woman and her son with glass objects, but they also blinded her boy by pouring nail polish remover into his eyes.

The young men then forced her and her son to lay naked in a bathtub together, and attempted to set them on fire. Thankfully, they could not find matches. The 10 youths then boldly took cell phone pictures of them so that they could enjoy their heinous acts at a later time. The torturous acts of violence continued for more than three hours.

To make matters worse, neighbors reported that they heard her screams, yet no one called the police or came to her aid. The Black woman and her son had to walk a mile to the hospital, because the predators stole her car, and threatened to kill her and her family if she told the police.

Then there's the 11-year old Black female minor who was brutally gang raped by 20 boys and men ranging from 13 to 40 years in age and the 16-year-old girl who helped set it up. Are these stories examples of hate crimes? Of course they are. But, what if it's not twenty men but one instead? What if the predator is not a stranger but a family member? Is it any less of a hate crime? I don't think so.

Unfortunately, domestic violence and sexual abuse are all too familiar to women in the Black community. The stories are plentiful but they are rarely told. The subject of sexual abuse, incest, rape, statutory rape and sexual assault are very ugly and hush hush topics amongst African-Americans. So many young women have been forced to suffer in silence while their own fathers, uncles, ministers, neighbors and countless others have used their penises as instruments of control to violate them. While victims live in torment, most abusers go unpunished.

How does this happen? It's simple. There seems to be very little value placed on Black female life. Just consider each possible scenario. After being raped, molested and assaulted, Black women are often manipulated by family and friends not to press charges. They are comforted but discouraged from seeking justice. They are taught to protect their predator because Black men are generally oppressed and unfairly treated by the legal system.

Even when the victim is a minor, there are parents who never report the assault to the authorities. So while these young Black girls are unprotected, their very own flesh and blood conceal the sexual crime and become protectors of those who prey upon them. In some cases, mothers are aware that their daughters are being sexually abused but turn a blind eye because the mother may benefit from the relationship with the abuser.

The female victim is typically not supported in her recovery or healing process, because to offer that support, would require the family to step out of their state of denial, thus making them acknowledge what really happened. In many cases the absence of the father denies the victim the much needed protection from sexual predators that she deserves. To top it off, civil rights organizations may rush to the defense of the predators to ensure that the legal system doesn't unfairly treat them.

So who can you turn to for help? Where can you go if the very ones who profess to love you turn a blind eye? Countless Black women continue to suffer on a daily basis because the support system that women of other cultures receive is not as prevalent within the Black community. While interviewing for this book project, several women shared their personal stories of abuse and abandonment.

I was molested at the age of 7 by my mother's boyfriend and my mother whooped me for telling her. Then at the age of 15 I was raped by my youth minister at my church. Then once again at the age of 25 my uncle tried to sexually assault me. I woke up to find him on top of me. I was married very young to a man who not only cheated with all the women in our church but also hit me repeatedly until he almost took my life. I don't know if I will ever truly heal from these situations but I am a little stronger each day. I fear for my daughters every day and I pray they never experience anything I have went through.

Brandy 33, Trainer

I was sexually assaulted by a friend and subsequently raped on two separate occasions by two other friends...all in undergrad. I never received support because I never told anyone and felt that it was my fault that these things happened to me. I carried it around with me for more than a decade, sabotaging relationships and myself because I felt unworthy to be loved. I've been in therapy for more than a year now trying to address these issues and rebuild my self-esteem so that I can have a successful relationship and life.

Janice, 41, Teacher

I was raped by a family member. Because we both were young, I received a "whoopin'" and was told that it was my fault. Also, I was told that I should have known better. My mother was in denial about it then, and she still may be.

Shanice, 36, Medical Technician

I was sexually abused growing up. I know for a fact that I was a very small child when it began with me and didn't stop until I was 10 or 11 years of age. And nobody really knows. The reason is that I was brought up in an era that no matter what the truth may be, if an adult say it's a lie then that's what it is "a lie". So that is one secret I have kept to myself up until I became an adult and had a breakdown and confided in my best friend and boyfriend at the time.

Yvonne, 46, Food Services

Too many Black women have suffered in silence because their mothers and fathers, friends and family, counselors and police, and the community at large have all devalued and blamed them. Sadly, the Black community has raised women to embrace a 'gender silence' which doesn't allow them to speak out against maltreatment based on gender. They can only vocalize their true voice within the arena of racial injustice and intolerance. This social imbalance serves to keep women forever trapped within the cells of their own minds, bodies, and relationships.

My Skin Is My Sin

When the topic of race is discussed, the conversation typically focuses on the plight of Black men. Black women are often an afterthought. The same is true for women's issues. White women are first considered then Black women. In essence, Black is equated with Black men and 'woman' is equated with White

20

women. So, Black women have always taken a back seat to both race and gender which have made them invisible in many respects. But reports would indicate that they are the most affected within each category.

In a June 2002 Gallup poll, 61 percent of Black women said they were dissatisfied with the treatment of Blacks in this society. The rate of dissatisfaction for Black men was 47 percent. Likewise, in the same poll, 48 percent of Black women versus 26 percent of

White women said they were dissatisfied with how women are treated in society. In both categories Black women faced greater dissatisfaction than both their male and female counterpart.

It must be made very clear that Black women are just as affected by race as Black men. If you're not convinced, consider the following true story.

A Black woman from Kennett, Missouri is currently facing 15 years in prison for cutting a line in a local Wal-Mart store. It all started nearly three years ago. Heather Ellis, a young college student, was shopping in the store with a cousin and the two parted ways to find the shortest line to purchase their items. When Ellis noticed the line her cousin was standing in was moving faster, Ellis went to get in line with her cousin (Don't we all do this? I know I do)!

Moments later, she was accused of cutting the line by a store employee, who then notified the security guard. Allegedly, Ellis was shoved by another customer, had her items pushed to the side and was shortchanged when she finally checked out. An argument ensued between Ellis and the employees of Wal-Mart.

The police affidavit stated that she became belligerent, loud, and verbally abusive when told to leave the store by the assistant manager. While cursing, a police officer grabbed Ellis and escorted her to his patrol car and repeatedly slammed her head against the roof of the car as she frantically cried for help saying "I wasn't resisting arrest."

When Ellis's aunt, a correctional officer, arrived to the scene she immediately inquired about the incident. All the officer could say was "She cursed." Ellis was later charged with disturbing the peace, trespassing, resisting arrest and two counts of assaulting a police officer. She was offered a plea deal by the county prosecutor along with reduced charges if she agreed to sign across the dotted line. The plea would keep her from suing the police department for the brutality she endured. She passed.

Eleven months later, the misdemeanor counts were dropped but they were replaced by felony counts. The prosecutor trumped up the charges because of her failure to comply with his plea bargain. So, cutting a line in a local store and choosing to not play ball with a corrupt justice system has put her at risk of facing 15 years in a prison camp. To make matters worse, members of the police department handed her Ku Klux Klan cards to "advise" her of what she might expect in the near future. The cards stated, "You've just been paid a social visit by the Ku Klux Klan; the next visit will not be social." The officer claims that he only showed the family the cards to make them aware of the situation. Yeah right!

According to annual reports from the Sentencing Project on crime and imprisonment in America, for the first time in American history Black women in some states are imprisoned at nearly the same rate as White men. They are jailed at even younger ages than ever before. While most arrests are due to admitted crimes, we would be naïve to think that none of the arrests were racially motivated.

Racial oppression towards women does not begin and end with the justice system. This oppression extends into many facets of life. The workforce is certainly one of those arenas. Within the workforce Black women are more likely to be unemployed or to take work for which they are over-qualified (Equal Opportunities Commission). According to *debthater.com*, Black women earn about 68 cents for every dollar White people earn. Even within high-paying corporate jobs there is a 'Black Tax' that exists which is the notion that African Americans have to work and perform regular tasks twice as well as White people for half the recognition. Although Black women have come a long way within the workforce, employer attitudes and prejudices still continue to hold our women back.

Women also suffer racism within the medical and health system. How many of you remember the Tuskegee Syphilis Experiment where Black men were used as laboratory animals? Between 1932 and 1972 (forty long years), the U.S. Public Health Service (PHS) conducted experiments and allowed hundreds of Black men to die of syphilis for research purposes.

Well, many of us are unaware of the sinister medical treatment Black women endured. Black women were routinely sterilized without their informed consent and for no valid medical reason. Teaching hospitals performed unnecessary hysterectomies on poor Black women as practice for their medical residents. This sort of abuse was so widespread in the South that these operations came to be known as 'Mississippi appendectomies.' In fact, 60 percent of the Black women in Sunflower County, Mississippi, were subjected to postpartum sterilizations at Sunflower City Hospital without their permission.

Crimes and injustices against Black women continue to be committed in every area of human relations. The educational, political, religious, legal, economic, medical and social systems of this nation have all contributed to the negative blows women endure on a daily basis. Unless these issues are brought to the forefront, women will continue to be victimized due to their race and gender.

Valuable Yet Not Valued
Black women in America have a very peculiar history. They have done so much to contribute to the world, yet have not been given their just due. The contributions of Abolitionists Harriet Tubman and Sojourner Truth, Inventor Madam C. J. Walker, Poet Maya Angelou, Entertainer Josephine Baker, Politician Shirley Chisholm, Activist Angela Davis, Actress Ruby Dee, Children's Advocate Marian Wright Edelman, Playwright Lorraine Hansberry, Organizer Dorothy Height, Singer Billie Holiday,

Why We Hate Black Women

Writer Bell Hooks, Astronaut Mae Jemison, Politician Maxine Waters, Athlete Jackie Joyner-Kersee, Civil Rights Activist Rosa Parks, Media Mogul Oprah Winfrey and other luminaries have certainly been acknowledged and celebrated.

But what about those faceless, voiceless Black women who work so hard and do so much and never receive any appreciation for their contribution? The treatment Black women have received in this country is reminiscent of how Africa has been treated throughout its history.

Africa has always been revered as the wealthiest continent on earth. It has given life, government, language, mathematics, science, culture and religion to the world. It is a landmass rich in African oil, African diamonds, African gold, African uranium, platinum, chrome, and gems such as emeralds, sapphires, rubies, and numerous other commodities, far too many to mention here.

But as rich as the land is, it has not enriched its people. Africa is a rich continent made poor by Western and European governments and corporations. They have successfully depleted the continent of trillions of dollars of its wealth. While these multi-national corporations rake in super profits, locals often live on $1 a day and left to starve and possibly die.

Overall, the people of Africa have been attacked and killed, and the land has been occupied, colonized and massively depleted of its natural resources by manifold nations. Well, Black women's experience in America parallels that dark history. Much like the continent, Black women are rich in treasures, gifts, talents and abilities that the world yearns for. Rather than being honored for their internal wealth, they have suffered a history of physical, sexual, emotional and reproductive exploitation at the hands of oppressors, who are legion.

In the words of Toni Morrison concerning Black women, "...she had nothing to fall back on; not maleness, not whiteness, not ladyhood, not anything. And out of the profound desolation of her reality she may well have invented herself." Morrison's words couldn't be any more true. Black women have been forced to become something they were never designed to be.

Too many Black women have been unprotected, exploited, abused, abandoned, and left to fend for themselves while being valued by no one. From the plantation to the present they have endured and overcome numberless harsh realities. In that process, they have transformed themselves to adjust to their less than desirable circumstances. In return, they have been further misunderstood and mistreated.

The remainder of this book will explore the state of Black women, their relationships, and their role in society. We will discuss their many strengths and weaknesses along with their accomplishments and setbacks. This manuscript wasn't written to be added to a collection of books on a shelf within your home. Rather, it was written to take you, the reader, on a mental journey. It is intended to challenge Black men and Black women to take an introspective look so that we may close the ever-increasing historical wedge in Black relationships and rebuild our families and our communities. Buckle Up!

Chapter 2

Too Strong For Your Own Good

Being a strong black woman is killing us softly.
~Unknown

*I*f it weren't for strong Black women where would we be today? The rich legacy of women like Sojourner Truth, Harriet Tubman, Ida B. Wells, Mary McCloud Bethune, Zora Neale Hurston, and Rosa Parks along with countless others is invaluable. Our race, as well as our nation, has benefited from the lives of these women and countless others.

But while the strength of Black women has done much for the Black community, it has created a multitude of problems within their personal lives. In fact, the Strong Black Woman persona has done more harm to Black women than good.

The 'Strong Black Woman' or 'Superwoman' personification has always functioned as a one-dimensional caricature. It is a depiction of a Black woman as a nurturer to the world and an unfeminine, strong willed, domineering brute to her man. In fact, the 'Strong Black Woman' has become the world's anti-example of femininity. Her physical, mental and emotional toughness has served to 'de-womanize' her in the eyes of the dominant culture. One brother said it plain, "femininity is dead among Black women." Whether he was aware or not, his statement spoke to the duality of sexism against Black women.

They have been made sexual objects and masculinized at the same time. Historically, their sexuality was rarely based upon their femininity. Rather, it was a tool for sexual exploitation at the hands of White men.

Beyond her objectified femininity was her ability to selflessly serve the world. She was pegged as the ultimate nurturer and has proven to be all things to all people, while neglecting her own needs. She has functioned as a mother, cook, care-giver, community organizer, culture bearer, and counselor. In fact, she's expected to cook every meal, attend every ball game, wipe every tear, support every family member, and do whatever is required to enhance the lives of those around her.

The tragedy is that with all of this strength, they are never given the opportunity to complain, cry, be vulnerable, seek sympathy or appear stressed. Unlike women of other nationalities, Black women are denied the luxuries of emotional breakdowns and failure. Black women who operate under the banner of 'Strength' often find it very difficult to get the empathy or compassion they seek. Their strength has overshadowed their gentleness, femininity, fragility and need to be cared for. In essence, they've exercised their super powers at the expense of their own happiness. And this is not a new phenomenon. It is a problem that has existed for centuries.

Black women have often been criticized for their strong personalities with no historical understanding as to how it all came to be. Widespread ignorance of their struggle has unfairly led to the assassination of their character. Though it may shock you, Black women did not come out of the womb strong. Black women in this country have a legacy of strength that dates back hundreds of years.

From slavery to modern times Black women have been taught to be strong while Black men have been systematically weakened. For instance, husbands were routinely burned, castrated, decapitated and lynched in the presence of their wives and children to reinforce the notion that Black men could not be depended on as protectors and providers of the family. Children were snatched from the arms of their mothers and sold off to other plantations. In certain southern states, Black babies were taken from mothers and used as alligator bait for White male hunters.

Black women not only suffered the loss of their loved ones but of their bodies as well. They were routinely raped, beaten, tortured, and dehumanized at the hands of their oppressor. The inhumane treatment that they all suffered created a sense of fear, trauma and the expectation of abandonment. As a result, the slave mother raised her male children to appear mentally weak in order to protect them from White slaughter. Meanwhile, her female children were raised to be strong in order to endure rape, torture and the loss of family.

The parenting style that began on the plantation is securely in place today. Even though Black men aren't physically lynched and castrated anymore, the woes of low educational obtainment, high unemployment, imprisonment, and dire economic hardship have stripped them of their role as protector and provider of the home. From slavery to the Antebellum Period, Reconstruction, Jim Crow, and the Civil Rights Era, the social climate has served to systematically weaken Black men thus changing the relational dynamic of the home.

Black women became the primary protector, provider and nurturer of the home. As a result, a gender power shift took place placing women in the seat of authority. Such conditions have significantly altered the parent/daughter conversation within the home. Just think about the messages that are reinforced in a family setting.

Whether by instruction or observation, most Black women have been taught to be self-reliant within their homes. The lesson they received was clear. 'Be strong and independent...Do for yourself...Don't rely on a man...Get your own this...Have your own that...Take care of yourself.'

Meanwhile, many young Black girls grew up in low income households which in turn forced them to grow up too fast. Many have taken on adult-like responsibilities, including contributing to the household financially while simultaneously filling the role of a second-mother to younger siblings while the mother struggled to make ends meet. These experiences have helped to shape young girl's attitudes and behavior about Black womanhood.

These lessons, which were birthed out of unfortunate circumstances, became the standard by which all lessons were taught. While parents meant well, they left their daughters with an incomplete teaching: 'Do for yourself'. The instructions were so focused on how to live independent of a man that they seldom learned how to properly function within a relationship. So, often times, when a relationship forms, conflict is inevitable.

Admittedly, many Black women suffer in silence today because of the strength they inherited from their mothers. While they are thankful for what it has allowed them to accomplish in society, it is one of many root causes of conflict in their relationships with Black men. In retrospect, many of these women wished they were taught when to cry and when to fight back their tears; when to show their vulnerabilities and when to be strong; when to ask for help instead of relying on their own strength.

Unfortunately, this legacy of strength has not only been passed down from slavery and taught in the home, it has been reinforced in society. This legacy of strength has ultimately spawned a newfound independence in many of our women.

The Strong Black INDEPENDENT Woman

Have you or someone you know ever muttered these words: "I'm a strong Black woman." "I can take care of myself." "I'm an independent woman." "I don't need a man to raise my kids."

In the minds of many women, these statements are a testament to the inner strength, power and resilience of Black women. Black men, on the other hand, receive a very different message. They often interpret these statements as "She doesn't want me, and she certainly doesn't need me, so, if she can do it all by herself, then she should be by herself." Whether perceived as good or bad, independence has caused a wedge in many African American relationships.

According to *Roget's Super Thesaurus*, synonyms for the word 'independent' include self-determining, self-governing, self-reliant, self-sufficient, and separate. Likewise, the word 'dependent' means to rely upon for support, and to place trust or confidence in. When these operational definitions are truly considered it delivers a very powerful message.

Women who remain committed to being independent within their relationships often leave men with no role to play. In essence, what they are really saying is, "I don't trust you...I don't have confidence in you...I will not rely on you...I'm going be self-determined, self-governing and self-sufficient." That attitude works as long as you are separate and not in a relationship. However, it challenges the foundation of a healthy relationship when both partners seek to fulfill very specific roles.

Neither men nor women should be independent within a relationship. It can never work. A healthy relationship requires interdependence which is a mutual dependency upon one another. Generally, men get into relationships because they want to be wanted, needed, trusted and relied upon. However, when women are asked to relinquish all forms of independence within their relationships it's often a very hard pill to swallow. Many of these women have had bad or absolutely no relationship with their fathers, brothers, baby-daddies and husbands. This has forced them to handle life's responsibilities alone.

So, when someone is used to supporting themselves, holding down one or more jobs, raising children, attending school, taking care of household expenses, paying bills and assisting other extended family members all by themselves, trading in independence for love seems both hard to comprehend and difficult to act out. This is hard, not so much because women don't want to but because they have little reference of it working.

The absence of men in their lives has taught them one very clear message. In order to get things done you can't trust or rely on a man. Even when a man is physically present, too many have failed to live up to their responsibilities. Why? Many men have grown up without a father and the lack of fatherhood often presents two main problems.

First, fatherlessness produces gender-role confusion. The responsibilities and obligations that a father would normally handle have instead been fulfilled by the mother. Therefore, a male child grows up seeing and believing that a woman is supposed to take care of everything because that's what he saw his mother do. As an adult, when he enters into a relationship, he's no help to a woman which ultimately makes her responsible for EVERYTHING.

Second, the lack of fatherhood contributes to a false definition of manhood. Rather than the father instructing the son on what it takes to be a real man, his understanding of manhood is shaped by the media, society and peers. Many men don't know how to truly treat and care for a woman because they never saw their father treat and care for their mother. As a result, this harsh reality has fueled the 'I don't need a man. I can do it all by myself' disposition that so many women have embraced.

While no woman should ever be forced to deal with a man who doesn't handle his responsibilities, her overall independence of a man often comes at a cost. Many have experienced lost opportunities with potential partners. Having the capacity to be independent when required is an admirable quality; however, making the decision to function independent of your partner presents an array of problems.

When a woman asserts her independence within a relationship, not only is she rejecting those who want to provide for her, but she is also rejecting those men who would like to cater to her as well. I have met countless women in my travels who have exhibited such a high level of independence that they refused to allow any man to buy them a meal, gifts, pay for a date, or give them anything of monetary value. I have seen them balk at the sight of a man pulling out a chair, opening up a car door or simply assisting with a coat before exiting a building.

As extreme as the previous examples may be, there are countless independent women who have been taught to guard themselves from such forms of chivalry. Complying with such acts would deem them weak and needy in a world where women are expected to be strong. On the other hand, there are independent women who would willingly accept any display of chivalry without the least bit of hesitation.

Interestingly, this whole 'independent crusade' which was birthed on the plantation and passed down from within the home has now become mainstream. When you listen to the lyrics of Hip Hop and R&B artists Webbie, Ne-Yo, Kanye West, and the like, they all express their desire to be with an independent woman who has her own house, car, and money. Songs like Destiny Child's *Independent Woman*, Ne-Yo's *Miss Independent*, Webbie's *I-N-D-E-P-E-N-D-E-N-T*, and Jamie Foxx's collaboration *She Got Her Own* all imply that her independence relinquishes her need for a man.

While these smooth groovin' tunes celebrate a woman's ability to take care of herself, they also deliver a message that challenges the presumed roles men and women have always been expected to play in society. As stated earlier in the chapter, it fuels the 'pretty men and working women' phenomenon. Ultimately, a woman's independence, as expressed in these songs, creates frustration in the woman and complacency in the man.

Beyond the lackadaisical disposition that these messages can potentially breed in men, the major problem with the independent woman profile is that she doesn't appear to have any needs or problems. A very one-dimensional character is portrayed. She's beautiful, her money's right, her hair's tight, and she possesses all of the luxuries that any man could ever give her.

The dilemma with this media glorified caricature is that in 3 ½ minutes flat the song is over. The lights are dimmed, the crew disperses and the set disappears. Meanwhile, strong Black independent women deal with all of the harsh realities of this world alone: escalating debt, overdue bills, crying babies, deadbeat dads, daycare challenges, multiple shift work, school, work deadlines, sleepless nights, needy family members, and the list goes on and on.

Is it too much for women to admit that they are in need of help? Does it make you any less of a woman if you acknowledge that you can't successfully do it all by yourself? Black women are making it, but they're frustrated and tired.

Just because you can feed a family with 3 boxes of Oodles of Noodles, bullion and some hot water doesn't mean your kids are nourished. Just because you can pay the electric company just in time to keep your lights from being turned off doesn't mean that you're financially secure. Just because you teach your son how to pee straight in the toilet without getting the seat wet doesn't mean he doesn't need a man in his life.

In our community the verbal acknowledgment of a woman's need for help has somehow been repackaged and falsely defined as 'needy'. This cultural LIE, which originates in pride, is one of several factors that have caused our women and children to suffer unnecessarily.

Socially conscious singer Jill Scott serenades her fan base with her own musical rendition of what it means to be a strong Black independent woman titled *The Fact Is (I Need You)*. The following is one verse of her song:

> I could be a congresswoman or a garbage woman
> or police officer or a carpenter
> I could be a doctor and a lawyer
> and a mother and a "good God, woman what chu
> done to me?" kind of lover I can be
> I could be a computer analyst
> The queen with the nappy hair raising her fist
> or I could be much more and a myriad of this
> Hot as the summer

Sweet as the first kiss
And even though I can do all these things
I need you
And even though I can do all these things
We need you
we need you
we need you
(and you need us too!)
              Jill Scott

According to women I have interviewed, Jill Scott's lyrics take a realistic approach to the heart and mind of most women. Women are strong enough, brave enough, competent enough, and diverse enough to perform the tasks of men. However, their ability should not be used to justify the replacement of his role and responsibility within the family.

For centuries Black women have been penalized for fulfilling a role that countless men have failed to play. Regardless of what B.E.T., urban radio stations, peers and even parental teachings have to say about the need for independence, it's important to understand there are appropriate and inappropriate times to demonstrate it. A balanced approach to independence can be a very helpful thing. However, the misuse of independence can be detrimental to all parties involved.

From Super Woman to Woman

A few years ago my wife and I attended a 2-day marriage retreat at a beautiful resort destination in Lancaster, Pennsylvania. During one of the seminars, husbands and wives were asked to name one quality about their spouses that they deeply admired. One-by-one partners named an admirable quality about their significant other. The activity was designed to be used as an icebreaker before the main teaching session; however, what started out as light-hearted soon became profound.

A newly-wedded couple shared their descriptions with the group. While the husband's remarks were sweet, the wife's statement was hard-hitting. She said, "What I love about my husband is that he is a good man and because of that I no longer have to be STRONG." Once she said it, it almost knocked me off my seat.

Here was a woman who spent most of her adult life raising kids, holding down a job, paying bills, and handling all of life's responsibilities alone. She played the role of mommy and daddy, protector, provider, caregiver, and was forced to wear a host of hats that didn't naturally fit. But, once she said 'I Do' she was willing to relinquish the reigns and hand them over to someone else.

In essence, she was saying I'm tired of playing the role of 'The Strong Black Woman.' I want to be taken care of for once. I want to be pampered and supported. I want the tears wiped from my eyes in my moment of weakness. I want to be free to be imperfect. I want to have my needs met without being labeled as needy. I want to be looked at as feminine and not hard. I want to embrace my strengths but also acknowledge my vulnerabilities. I want to be free to be me and not imprisoned behind bars that define my existence in a one-dimensional way.

The bottom line is that no woman can ever be a COMPLETE human being while trying to be strong and hard their entire lives. The creation of the 'superwoman' persona has left many women cheated out of a life of normalcy. Instead, they've played the role of superhero to the Black community. The Black "superwoman" shoulders burdens and shares attributes in common with comic book heroes like Superman, Batman, and Spiderman. Consider the list of similarities:

1) <u>Self Sacrificing</u> – All superheroes possess a strong moral code, including a willingness to risk one's own safety in exchange for the good of the people. Many Black women

have been the caregiver for so long that they've neglected their own health, happiness and well-being.

2) Tragic Past- Most superheroes have experienced elements of tragedy in their past which have in turn triggered their new role as hero/heroine. Batman suffered the loss of his parents at the hands of a street thug. Spiderman's close uncle was murdered by a thief Spiderman had failed to capture. Likewise, countless Black women have a tragic past (fatherlessness, teen parenthood, rape and molestation, watching their mothers being abused and/or relationship issues) which have resulted in the hardening of their personas and have led to their role of being 'Strong, Black and Independent.'

3) Super Powers and Abilities – Superheroes either possess extraordinary powers and abilities (superhuman strength, the ability to fly, and enhanced senses) or have mastered certain skills (martial arts, forensic science, and technology) that have allowed them to overcome their opposition. Likewise, Black women have mastered the skill of playing dual roles, running a household, being the sole provider, managing finances, and a long list of other tasks through which she demonstrates that she is a superwoman.

4) Secret Identity - Superheroes who maintain a secret identity often wear a mask, covering the upper face, leaving the mouth and jaw exposed. This allows for both a believable disguise and recognizable facial expressions. A notable exception is Superman, who wears nothing on his face while fighting crime, but uses large glasses in his civilian life as Clark Kent. In most cases, the hero persona is an alter-ego of the human reality. Likewise, there are Black women who metaphorically wear the mask. Their true identity and nature is often hidden behind a need to portray a life of strength, self-reliance and infallibility.

African American poet Paul Laurence Dunbar wrote, "WE wear the mask that grins and lies, It hides our cheeks and shades our eyes, - This debt we pay to human guile; With torn and bleeding hearts we smile, And mouth with myriad subtleties. Why should the world be over-wise, In counting all our tears and sighs? Nay, let them only see us, while We wear the mask."

In addition to the physical mask and costume used to hide the identity of the hero, is the masking of the hero's true desires. Anyone who knows anything about superheroes is well aware that they are trapped within their own prison. In other words, they all get to a point when they no longer want to fulfill the role as hero. They're tired of saving the day and coming to everyone's rescue. Sometimes they get weary. Sometimes they want to ignore the injustice just to have a sense of normalcy. Strong Black women often admit that their strength is a trap that pulls them right back into a role that they desperately want to do away with.

5) <u>Public Disdain</u> – Heroes like Batman, Spider-Man, and the X-Men are often met with public skepticism and hostility. They defend a populace that misunderstands and despises them. Black women have not only been strong for themselves but for others as well. Unfortunately, their greatest strength (the need to be strong) has become their greatest weakness in the eyes of others. Therefore, they are often criticized by the world and rejected by their own men for the role they've been forced to play.

6) <u>Failed Relationships</u> - Most superheroes struggle in the area of romance. Every time they gain a love interest, something always goes terribly wrong. They're often faced with the dilemma of choosing between two worlds: the world of heroism in order to fight injustice and the world of mortality in order to pursue love.

In the movie *Dark Knight (2008)*, Batman was prepared to give up his role as protector of Gotham City in order to settle down with his love interest Rachel. Unfortunately, she was maliciously killed by the Joker. Spiderman was in love, and engaged to Mary Jane Watson, but had to end the relationship in order to fulfill his role as protector to the world. In *Superman II (1980)*, Superman gave up his superpowers and became a mere mortal in order to marry Lois Lane. But once Superman realized the world was in danger, he ended the relationship and reacquired his powers for the sake of world peace.

Lastly, in Hancock (2008), Will Smith's character lost his super powers and faced near death every time he made contact with his female counterpart Mary Embrey. In order to stay safe from harm, Hancock and Mary were forced to remain separate from one another. In fact, the further apart they were the more supernatural strength they each possessed.

In every case these heroes were forced to trade in their happiness, personal fulfillment and pursuit of a romantic relationship for what their powers designated them to be and do. The personal tragedy of most heroes is that they often live a very lonely and unfulfilled life. Their gift to the world has placed them in a prison of isolation.

Sadly, countless strong Black independent 'superwomen' have found themselves like most superheroes: alone and relationally unfulfilled. Unfortunately, while the strength of Black women has done much to contribute towards the advancement of the Black community, it has created a multitude of problems in the personal lives of Black women. As mentioned earlier in the chapter, the 'superwoman' persona has done more harm to Black women than good.

So, for all Black women who have fallen into this trap, it's time to take the 'S' off of your chest and give up this false definition of strength.

The High Price of Strength

Every time I hear a sistah brag about being a 'Strong Black Woman' I get extremely annoyed. I'm annoyed that no other cultural group of women wears 'strength' as a badge of honor except Black women. I'm annoyed that the expression of a woman's strength is often clothed in bitterness and frustration. I'm annoyed that our culture glorifies this handcrafted concept of a 'Strong Black Woman' as something that should be celebrated rather than redefined.

I'm annoyed because it lets millions of Black men off the hook. Why step up, as men, and be strong if our women have already sworn a die-hard allegiance to it? I'm annoyed because it keeps women trapped in a prison that they desperately want to get out of, though many have refused to admit it. I'm annoyed because it has forced so many Black women to live in complete denial.

That's right! You read it correctly. Strong Black Women or 'Superwomen' are in complete DENIAL. Now, before you get offended by my statement please consider what I am actually saying. *The American Heritage College Dictionary* defines the word 'denial' in a multitude of ways which include, a) a refusal to acknowledge one's own painful reality, thoughts and feelings, b) a refusal to accept the truth for what it is, and c) a refusal to satisfy one's own personal needs. Truth be told, Strong Black Women are guilty of all of the above.

First, this unhealthy relationship with strength has forced Black women to refuse to acknowledge their own painful realities, thoughts and feelings. Whenever faced with difficulties and challenges, 'Strong Black Women' respond with the same old mantra, "I'm strong enough, I'm tough enough, I can handle it, and I've got everything under control." And to their credit, our families and our communities survived. However, sistahs pay a heavy price every time they play savior to the world.

They lose touch with who they really are. In fact, they execute a self protective strategy of appearing strong in order to hide their

40

feelings and emotions. Why? If they didn't, their cover would be blown. You see, they can't convince people of their strength if they have needs of their own. So strong women often refuse to open up and become vulnerable in order to retain the esteem of those around her.

This sick and twisted game promises to always keep 'Strong Black Women' in last place. It allows them to take care of others but forbids them from ever being reciprocated with the same much needed care. As mentioned earlier, 'Strong Black Women' have mastered the art of wearing the mask. But if you look close enough, you can see their tears full of pain, loneliness and heartbreak. Unfortunately, many women battle with stress, anxiety, depression and a host of other emotional health concerns because their emotional well being is totally neglected and denied.

Second, many women who hold onto the term 'strength' refuse to accept the truth behind its meaning. The words 'strong' or 'strength' have both positive and negative connotations. In one respect, strong is defined as secure, self-confident, resilient, and durable, while strength is defined as the ability to maintain a moral or intellectual position firmly and as the embodiment of protective or supportive power. There are countless Black women who represent these descriptions in its entirety.

Likewise, there's another group of adjectives that represent the negative expression of a woman's strength. Those words include hardened, severe, forthright and explicit, often offensively so; uncompromising, having an intense or offensive effect on the senses; and loud and harsh.

So, the concept of strength is a mixed-bag. While some sistahs convey their strength in a positive way, others are overwhelmingly negative in their expression. There are also women who express both its positive and negative characteristics. If women could somehow stop romanticizing the 'Strong Black Woman' personification and acknowledge its flaws and limitations and focus on its positive expression, it would significantly change women's relationships with men, society and themselves.

Third, 'Strong Black Women' live a life of self-denial. They refuse to comply with or satisfy their own needs. Author Debrena Jackson Gandy defines Black women's affliction as "our obsession with overworking, overextending ourselves, and over nurturing others." And sisters are tired. They're tired of always trying to please and putting everyone else's needs – husbands, lovers, children, employers, friends, family – before their own. They're tired of being last, yet they instinctively place everyone else first.

They often refuse to make self-care a priority. And I'm not talking about the occasional massage, manicure and pedicure. Everyone one gets that every now and then. I mean the intentional focus on their physical health, spirituality, and personal aspirations. Erica Lewis, an African American health and fitness consultant said it best:

"The independent black woman stigma has gone too far. As Black women I think we've put too much on our plate. We're managing our homes, our careers, and our lives and we're just doing way too many things. We're strong in an array of areas. However, we're weak with our own selves. We have high blood pressure, we're overweight. We're not taking care of our health, emotions, spirits and minds. We're not taking care of ourselves. But in the world's eyes we're this strong Black woman. We're too busy giving the strong black woman to the world and not ourselves."

Not only is Ms. Lewis' statement true, it's clearly played out in a variety of areas. Concerning health, the mortality rates for African-American women are higher than any other racial/ethnic group for nearly every major cause of death including diabetes, heart disease, lung cancer, cerebrovascular disease, breast cancer, and chronic obstructive pulmonary diseases.

Spiritually speaking, more emphasis should be placed on relationships rather than religion. A proper relationship with God will help women restore their souls, help redefine their purpose, and give them the balance they so desperately need in life. This will in turn help women achieve their personal aspirations which have always been trumped by the need to help everyone else first.

When women begin to consider that their 'strength' has contributed to the loss of their happiness, their health, their pursuits and their relationships, it may cause them to reevaluate and redefine the strength that they possess within their own lives. Within the proper context, strength can be a wonderful thing. Unfortunately, it can also lead to one's own detriment. However, when it is properly balanced it can be an asset to all parties involved.

Chapter 3

From The Auction Block To The Table Top

No other group in America has so had their identity socialized out of existence as have black women....
~Bell Hooks

lack women have had a very dark sexual history recorded within the annals of American life. From the moment they set foot on the shores of America, to their present day existence, Black women have been robbed of their femininity, physically raped and racially ridiculed by a system fueled by racial and gender oppression.

From the auction blocks of American plantations to the symbolic table-tops of White America's socially constructed Black-female-reality, Black women have been painted with several sexual broad strokes which have falsely defined their existence. While the oppression of Black men primarily focused on racial differences, White men's mistreatment of Black women was often undergirded with an unspoken sexual curiosity.

The false notion that Black women were naturally and inevitably sexually promiscuous was reinforced by the institution of slavery. Slave masters typically provided shabby clothing that often exposed women's legs, thighs and chests. This was a stark contrast from White women who wore clothing over most of their bodies. While clothing reinforced the belief that White women were civilized, modest and sexually pure, the enforcement of Black female nakedness implied a lack of civility, morality and sexual restraint.

With that in mind, the auctioning of slaves on an auction block further cheapened the sexuality of Black women. It represented the first place they began to lose their dignity. They were often stripped naked and physically examined. Publicly, it was done to ensure a slave's health, to check her ability to reproduce, and to identify whipping scars which implied a slave's willingness to rebel. In reality, the stripping and touching of female slaves fulfilled a sexual function.

Auctioneers and prospective buyers examined their teeth, pulled their eyelids back and gazed into their eyes; their tormentors manhandled them as if they were field animals. Their captors pinched their limbs to see how muscular they were. They were also forced to bend over so interested White men could check them for hidden wounds. They were made to run, jump and do many other humiliating tricks so the potential buyers could check for any lameness in them.

Often, they were taken away from the auction block to a small house in a secluded area where they were made to remove all their clothing for further inspection. It was used as a way to see if slaves were healthy and fit. In reality, it was nothing more than an opportunity to get a free plantation peep show.

Now, 390 years after slavery's inception, Black women are still for sale. Unfortunately, they have not been able to escape the stigma inherited from the plantation. Though slavery ended, capitalism continues on and a new market for Black women has been created. They are no longer being bought and sold as commodities on an auction block. However, negative images of Black women are being bought and sold in multiple arenas today.

Corporate movie and music executives, cable networks, record label companies, artists, and women themselves have sold a negative image of Black women to the highest bidder. Their bodies are for sale in both film and music videos, and they continue to be devalued and undervalued in the workplace and within the home.

While White men once monopolized the sexual exploitation of Black women, they have since spread the wealth by allowing Black men to profit from various acts of degradation as well. In essence, a symbolic nod has been given to willing African American male participants.

Black men, under the supervision of White corporate executives, have utilized Hip Hop as a vehicle to reinforce plantation-rooted stereotypes of Black women. The over-exposed depiction of sexual deviance has helped to further cement the negative imagery of Black women. With constant visual references of the Hip Hop stripper-ho, the table-top has become the modern day auction block. So, what was created almost 400 years ago on slave plantations can currently be seen in Hip Hop videos today.

Black women have suffered from a dark history which has theoretically taken them from an auction block to a table-top. When you compare the historic imagery created by White men with the contemporary recreation of those images perpetuated by Black men, you must ask yourself, "Just how different are these women?"

One was enslaved by her own sexuality. The other maintained a newfound sexual freedom. One drew the crowds of White men, while the other drew the crowds of Black men. One was chosen to work the field. The other was chosen to work a room. One suffered from forced nudity by being stripped of her clothing, while the other voluntarily embraced her nudity by taking off her own clothing. One was oiled down and made to appear healthy. The other oiled herself up to accentuate the beauty of her body.

One was beaten with a rod, while the other swung from a pole. One was constantly poked and prodded by potential buyers. The other was fondled and grouped by voyeuristic onlookers. One was sold for monetary gain. The other believed she was empowered because she willingly sold herself for monetary gain. So once again, I ask the question, "Just how different are these women?" As you ponder that thought, the more important question is, "What happened over a 390-year span that made such a similarity even possible?"

The dark reality is that what started on the plantation continued throughout the Antebellum Period, Reconstruction, Jim Crow, the Civil Rights Era, the Black Power Movement, all throughout the 80s and 90s and even into the new millennium. Throughout this span of time several stereotypical images were created to further demonize and exploit Black women. Each false characterization was deliberate and intentional in its creation. There was either an economic, political, social or sexual agenda involved which solely benefited the men who created such images. These stereotypical caricatures are broken into several female categories.

Mammy & Aunt Jemima

Mammy is the most recognizable and enduring racial caricature of African American women. Usually imagined as a large, older Black woman, this house servant was in charge of her master's children and domestic responsibilities such as cooking and cleaning. In the plantation house, the mammy was a caretaker, a housekeeper-maybe even a surrogate grandmother-and, for the most part, a myth.

From slavery through the Jim Crow Era, the mammy image served the political, social and economic interests of White America. The mammy caricature was created to offer undeniable proof that Blacks were content and happy to be slaves. In fact, mammy's grins and smiles solidified the notion that slavery was a decent and humane institution.

The mammy was depicted as a lover of all things White. She loved her White family. She loved raising her White surrogate children. She often treated her White family better than her own. She loved working in the big house next to White folks.

Beyond her obsession with White skin, the fictitious mammy image was created by White southerners in order to hide the sexual relationship between Black women and White men. One of the most painful aspects of the slave experience was the sexual exploits of White slave owners and their children, White over-seers, and other White male benefactors. This relationship also ushered itself into the post-slavery antebellum period. Therefore, all Black women and girls, regardless of their physical appearances, were vulnerable to being sexually assaulted by White men. While White women were placed on pedestals and epitomized as pure and sacred beings, White men secretly lusted after Black women. So the biggest lie that the mammy caricature told was that White men did not find Black women sexually desirable.

The mammy caricature was deliberately created to depict the sheer ugliness or unattractiveness of Black female slaves. Their attempt to desexualize the mammy image was very successful because they relied on a triple-whammy combination that made her totally undesirable: 1) she was dark-skinned, even pitch black, in a society where blackness was deemed as ugly 2) she was morbidly obese which would turn off any reasonable man and 3) she was old and beyond the age of attraction.

This very distorted image essentially stripped Black women of all of their sensual qualities. The presumption was that no (White) man would ever desire such a woman when compared to the idealized White woman. This, in turn, soothed the minds of White women who felt like Black women would lure weak-willed White men away and wreck their already turbulent home life. So, White men's ability to enjoy the sweet nectar of Black women (through massive rapes) was predicated on a far-reaching, morbid exaggeration of reality: the mammy.

According to Bell Hooks, "Considering white male lust for bodies of black females, it is likely that white women were not pleased with young black women working in their homes for fear that liaisons between them and their husbands might be formed, so they conjured up the image of the black nanny." This statement shows how White women felt threatened by African American women. This is because some White men were fascinated by African American females as they were looked upon as an exotic other. The mammy figure represented an asexual mother figure complete with over-exaggerated enlarged breasts and buttocks which symbolized womanhood, thus remaining outside the sphere of sexual desirability and into the realm of maternal nurturance.

The truth of the matter is that female house maids were anything but dark-skinned, over weight, large-breasted, handkerchief-wearing, nappy haired, sexless Black women. Real-life Black domestics during slavery and the Jim Crow era were young, slender and possibly fair skinned women. The tranquil, docile, happy ex-slave Black woman who only lived to serve White people's bottomless needs was also fictitious. On the contrary, many women forced to work in White people's homes resented their jobs and the realities that came along with it.

Meanwhile, the maintenance of the mammy myth affected both White Southern womanhood and Black Southern manhood. The idea of the strong Black matriarch carries with it the notion of power and dominance. The mammy role has been burdened with the accusation of robbing Black men of their manhood because of the matriarchal tradition that she exists in.

Eldridge Cleaver, in *Soul on Ice*, offered a contemporary analysis of sexual, racial and power relations in U.S. society:

"The myth of the strong black woman is the other side of the coin of the myth of the beautiful dumb blonde. The white man turned the white woman into a weak-minded, weak-bodied, delicate freak, a sexpot, and placed her on a pedestal; he turned the black woman into a strong, self-reliant Amazon and deposited her in his kitchen — that's the secret of Aunt Jemima's bandanna. The white man turned himself into the Omnipotent Administrator and established himself in the Front Office. And he turned the black man into the Super-masculine Menial and kicked him out into the fields."

Unfortunately, this caricature did not end with the emancipation proclamation. It became both a main staple and hallmark of American culture. The mainstreaming of mammy was the result of the advertising/commercial industry. The mammy image was used to sell almost any item imaginable: breakfast foods

(Aunt Jemima Pancakes), detergents, beverages, ashtrays, and sewing accessories. The image appeared on baking powder, coffee and cleaners. The success the mammy caricature experienced in the commercial industry was matched by Hollywood.

From Hollywood's *Birth of a Nation (1915), Gone With The Wind (1939), Song of the South (1946), to The Imitation of Life (1958),* the mammy was a familiar and reliable figure for American filmmakers. In fact, the mammy has persisted as one of the few recurring images of Black women on the screen. Actresses like Annie Johnson and Hattie McDaniel were commonly used to play such roles. Once they both passed away, the mammy role essentially disappeared from the screen.

The emergence of Black pride created a new market for films made specifically for Black audiences, and a shrinking market for films which perpetuated myths no longer acceptable due to the increasing social consciousness of the 60s and 70s. So the elimination of old stereotypes fostered the creation of new personae by such performers as Pam Grier, Diana Ross and Cicely Tyson. Now in 2010, some forty years after the entrance of the aforementioned actors graced the big screen, there has been a resurgence of the mammy role like never before.

From Mammy To Madea

Who decided that portraying brown/dark-skinned, heavyset women was supposed to be funny? Black comedic actors along with film industry executives have done a masterful job of perpetuating the negative stereotypical images of Black women. All you need is a floral housecoat, polyester pantsuit, a glass of cognac and a masculine attitude of aggression and you've got a hit on your hands. Several male actors have dabbled in or built a career with this demeaning genre of entertainment. It's a disgrace when Black America's leading ladies are really men.

Black men in drag have always been viewed as a deplorable and socially unacceptable practice within the Black community unless it's used to demean Black women. Unfortunately, there's a

51

long history of Black men dressing up in women's attire to portray loud, offensive, crude, ignorant and usually dark-skinned and obese Black women. With the freedom of artistic license, sisters have often become evil and ugly objects devoid of humanity. However, Black families across the nation continue to rush to the silver screen in order to get a front row seat as they watch the character assassination of Black women under the guise of entertainment.

In fact, some of the most memorable women in Black entertainment have been played by men. Consider the following list:
1. Flip Wilson's sassy Geraldine Jones
2. Jamie Foxx's cockeyed, man-chasing Wanda Wayne
3. Miguel A. Nunez Jr.'s *Juwanna Mann*
4. Martin Lawrence's sarcastic, ghetto-fabulous Sheneneh Jenkins
5. Martin Lawrence's stubborn, feisty matriarch, *Big Momma*
6. Eddie Murphy's super-sized, mean-spirited Rasputia in *Norbit*.
7. Tyler Perry's God-fearing, over-weight, gun-toting and cussin' Madea Simmons
8. Kenan Thompson's gluttonous, obtuse and ignorant Virginiaca,
9. And the list goes on and on...

Interestingly, according to Marjorie Garber's 1999 book, *Vested Interests*, the men who played women in minstrel shows were "the best-paid performers in the minstrel company." The same seems to be true today. Not only are some of these Black men the highest paid among male actors, they have made more money playing women than women have made playing themselves.

Martin Lawrence grossed $173,559,438 worldwide with a $33,000,000 budget for *Big Momma's House*. Lawrence grossed $137,047,376 worldwide with a $40,000,000 budget for *Big Momma's House 2*. Eddie Murphy grossed $158,973,607 worldwide with a $65,000,000 budget for *Norbit*.

Tyler Perry has made an astronomical $50 million writing and producing plays for an urban theater "chitlin'" circuit. Once he transitioned into silver screen production he grossed an impressive combined $130,000,000 worldwide for his first three movie projects. Meanwhile, cable network TBS bought his sitcom *House of Payne* for $200 million.

These three men have received big ticket sales and big studio budgets that dwarf the typical all Black cast movie production. There is an underlying message in these numbers. It says 'We'd rather see Black men play Black women, than Black women play themselves.'

Interestingly, in *Norbit*, the character Rasputia, a 400-pound, foul-mouthed, dark-skinned, ghetto-acting monstrosity of a woman, plays opposite of Thandie Newton, a soft-spoken, skinny, light-skinned bi-racial woman with European-styled hair and more Caucasian-like features. The stark contrast speaks to another already existing stereotype. Dark-skin is associated with being ugly, undesirable, uncouth, and uncivilized. Light skin is associated with being beautiful, desirable, and civilized. And when Hollywood does choose a Black woman who is "beautiful" they often choose women of mixed race such as Thandie Newton, Halle Berry, Vanessa Williams and so on. They're basically saying in order to be beautiful, you have to be anointed with White heritage.

The *Saturday Night Live* character Virginiaca, played by Kenan Thompson, portrays a ghetto, hyper-sexualized Black woman before a predominately White audience. Adding insult to injury, her daughter is played by a White woman in blackface, sporting a huge Black afro and an ebonics speech pattern. The entire skit is a modern day minstrel show--with mispronounced words, exaggerated outfits, big hair, and a whole lot of dancing.

Unfortunately, African Americans' welcoming acceptance of these Black female caricatures have paved the way for White men to follow suit. Arkansas City Mayor Mel Kuhn, of Arkansas appeared in full mammy tradition when he appeared in blackface as part of a municipal court sponsored drag-queen beauty contest. His dark makeup, oversized frame, vulgar character name "Smellishis Poon", referring to female genitalia, along with his back up dancers 'The Red Hot Puntangs' danced to 'black music':

The Weather Girls and Aretha Franklin. Ultimately, he won the weekend fundraiser.

The mayor told *The Arkansas City Traveler* newspaper that he got the idea for the character from the movies *Norbit* and *Big Momma's House*, which feature Black men portraying Black women. He said painting his face and portraying a Black woman 'was the best way to win.' "I had to make it as funny as possible. That was the best way I could think of to make as many people laugh as possible and raise money for this charity. After being criticized by the NAACP for racist portrayal, he said that he did not really manage to carry out the character as a Black woman. To add further insult to injury he said, "I can't do a Black accent," he said. Wow.

Whether the impersonator is Black or White really makes no difference. At the end of the day, Black women are the butt of all jokes gone wrong. Whether the mammy character is done in poor taste or with a sense of cultural sensitivity, the asexual, overweight, dark-skinned and domineering stereotype continues to stain the life and legacy of Black women in America.

Jezebel

The Jezebel stereotype is the representation of an erotically appealing temptress and openly seductive, promiscuous woman with an insatiable sexual appetite. The name Jezebel has become synonymous with women who engage in lewd sexual acts and who take advantage of men through sex. This stereotype is one of the main ways White America views Black women. It is why so many think Black women are loose, immoral and oversexed.

This caricature is the one stereotype that predates the plantation. The notion of Black women as sexually loose began to materialize from the moment that Europeans hit the shores of Africa.

Black women were exported from Africa to America by White men to work in the south and breed a large slave population to enhance the workforce with free labor. Not only did these men control the labor of Black women and their offspring children, they also controlled Black women's bodies through rape. If a female slave became pregnant by her master, she was punished with her mulatto offspring being sold off to hide his sexual indiscretions from his wife and the rest of society.

A slave who refused the sexual advances of her owner or overseer risked being sold, beaten, raped, and having her husband or children sold. So, in exchange for their cooperation they were sometimes promised food, the safety of their children, or to be treated less harshly on a day to day basis. With such limited choices, Black women had no other option but to succumb to White men's desires or face severe punishment.

The sexual relationship between Black women and White men was so common that author Andrea Williams wrote, "Perhaps she remembers her great-great grandmother who wanted to protest but only rolled her eyes and willed herself not to scream when the White man mounted her from behind." This was an unfortunate but common practice on the plantation. As a result, their forced sexual submissiveness further strengthened the jezebel stereotype of Black women as lascivious.

So, White men created the jezebel stereotype to rationalize the widespread rape of Black women. Driven by their desire to dominate Black women through rape, or motivated by simple sexual attraction, White men would engage in sexual intercourse, and subsequently blame this act on the very Black women they sexually exploited. They created a widespread lie that Black women had an insatiable appetite for sex that could not be satisfied by Black men. It was claimed that she desired sexual relations with White men; therefore White men did not have to rape Black women. Because Black women were property, they legally could not be raped anyway.

In addition to the sexual role Black women had to play with White men, they were expected to fulfill the same role with Black men. Since slavery depended upon Black women to supply future slaves, they were often pregnant. Owners often offered slaves a new pig for each child born to a slave family, a new dress to the female for each surviving infant, or no work on Saturdays to Black women who birthed six or more children. In this slave system, young Black girls were often encouraged to have sex. While they weren't expected to give birth, they were made to succumb to a forced socialization that would guarantee their role as a breeder once they became of age. If they did reproduce, it was viewed as proof of their insatiable desire for sex which further played into the Jezebel role.

Defined through this Jezebel caricature, Black women were objectified and became fetishes associated with alluring but exaggerated large breasts, large buttocks, and smiling faces. Faces of young girls were even displayed featuring adult sized buttocks wrapped in seductive attire. Common items designed for purchase were even made to brand a stereotypical depiction of her nakedness and body type. Ashtrays, sheet music, drinking glasses, postcards and a variety of other items portrayed scantily clad Black women. They went as far as creating a nutcracker where the nut would be placed under the skirt, in her crotch and crushed. It was done to show that Black women lacked humility, decency and sexual restraint.

Once slavery ended, Black women were physically free but still sexually bound to negative imagery and forced sexual behavior. The Emancipation and Reconstruction did not stop the sexual victimization of Black women. In fact, from the end of the Civil War to the mid-1960s, no White male was convicted of raping or attempting to rape a Black woman.

Jezebel Goes To Hollywood

Beyond this harsh reality, a well-funded propaganda machine was created which further exploited the false notion of Black female sexuality. The oversexed representations of Black women continually bombard the media as the most accurate portrayal of African-American women. From Hollywood films to music videos, images of immoral and loose Black women dominate the silver screen and all other forms of media outlets. So, the media took the widely accepted jezebel myth of the past, and transformed it into the contemporary oversexed Black female actress.

Early on in American film, the influences of the jezebel are apparent. After the mammies ran its course by the 1950s, the hypersexual Black female replaced her as the dominant stereotype of Black women in American culture. From Dorothy Dandridge to Josephine Baker, Pam Grier, and Hale Berry many Black women have been typecast, forced to depict the Jezebel stereotype and publicly praised in the process.

Dorothy Dandridge gained success by playing characters like *Carmen Jones (1954)*, a promiscuous woman who met her demise, as a result, of her whorish ways. Despite her attempt to present a broader view of Black women through her performances in over twenty-eight films, she was given an Oscar Nomination only when she returned to her role as a sexual play toy which was a role that perpetuated stereotypes of Black females. It wasn't until she played a whore (Bess) in *Porgy and Bess (1959)* that she received a Golden Globe Award as Best Actress.

As the seventies appeared, Black female roles continued to reflect the same hyper-sexualized image of Black women. The Blaxploitation era was successful at modernizing the Jezebel image. These primarily Black casted movies were produced by White film companies in an attempt to empower Black people. Instead, White male producers typecast Black women as concubines, prostitutes, and superb-tches—roles that were just as profitable as they were damaging.

Actress Pam Grier reinforced the jezebel stereotype with such films like *Coffy, Foxy Brown,* or *Sheba, and Baby.* Her scantily clad attire, sexual and violent acts and nudity fostered traditional beliefs about Black women as immoral and lewd. Pam Grier, much like Dorothy Dandridge in the fifties and sixties, was only awarded for her acting when she played a character that confirmed these false stereotypes of Black women.

After a long tradition of Black female actresses playing jezebel roles, Halle Berry's lucrative film career took off after her sexually graphic performance in Monster's Ball. Decades after Dorothy Dandridge was nominated for an Academy Award for playing a consummate whore in Carmen Jones, Halle Berry became the first Black woman to win the coveted Best Actress Oscar award. In reality, the Academy awarded Berry for Hollywood's best sexual performance ever conducted on film which was a historical reminder of Black women's true role as sexual deviants. In the movie, she asked Thorton's White character to "make her feel better." They then performed one of the rawest, most intense sexual scenes in American cinematic history. And Berry received enormous amounts of news coverage for her role as an erotic and sexually loose woman who slept with a White man she barely knew.

Interestingly, the depiction of Black women's sexual relationship with White men on film is nothing new. Dorothy Dandridge starred in four films with this unique sexual tie. Lola Falana (Emma Jones) played a concubine of a White man in *The Liberation of L.B. Jones (1970)*. Lisa Bonet, one of the daughters on the *Cosby* show, played a voodoo priestess in *Angel Heart* (1987) opposite Mickey Rourke. The movie was perceived as so graphic that it almost received an X rating. In *Harlem Nights* (1989), Sunshine (played by Lela Rochon) is a prostitute so skilled that a White lover calls his wife on the telephone to tell her that he is never returning home. The list of films is so great that it goes beyond the scope of this book.

As you can see, just as White men exploited Black women's bodies as breeders during slavery, film executives followed in the same tradition of sexual exploitation by making movies that capitalized on Black women's seemingly "whorish" nature. So, the Black female body rendered a significant economic reward. From the plantation to the big screen, the false hypersexual image of Black women was packaged, financed and sold at a profit largely by White men. Unfortunately, the century-long legacy remains.

TRAGIC MULATTO

The Tragic Mulatto is a close cousin of the Jezebel caricature. They are similar in that they both share the reputation of being sexually seductive. However, the mulatto is often physically depicted as a fair-complexioned woman with thin lips, a slender nose, long straight hair, and a thin figure. This woman is also referred to as mulatta, mongrel, spurious, and high yella as a result of her pale skin tone. She is viewed as a female with both Black and White parents and the birth of this caricature can be traced all the way back to the sexual abuse of female slaves on the plantation. Black women were often abused and raped by their White slave authorities (whether masters or overseers).

The tragedy in the forced sexual relationship of female slaves was the birth of mix-raced children in a slave system where it would be extremely difficult to find acceptance in both communities. In Hollywood the female mulatto was portrayed as one who was ignorant of both her mother's race and her own and believed herself to be White and free.

Her life was spent trying to pass as White but once her Negro blood was discovered she was forced back into slavery where she was neither accepted by the White or Black community, which resulted in her demise.

The Tragic Mulatto's challenge was that an interracial offspring was always legally regarded as pure Black no matter what their physical appearance may suggest. To be truly White, one had to be all White. Therefore, the mulatto's White heritage gave her no real advantage towards a life of freedom. In fact, her racial blend made her prone to more attack. Mulatto women were often targeted for sexual abuse. In slave markets they were bought at higher prices, simply because of their use as sexual objects. While dark skin was considered vulgar and repulsive, mulattos were a reminder of the White ideal of female attractiveness.

Symbols of rape and concubinage, mulattos were viewed as seducers whose beauty was so striking that they often drove White men to sexually crave them thus resulting in a legacy of rape. The constant sexual domination of mulatto slaves resulted in the creation of several mixed-breeds such as quadroons, octoroons and quintroons. These labels were racial categories used to describe proportions of African ancestry in mixed-race people in slave societies.

Quadroon usually referred to someone of one-quarter Black ancestry; that is, with three White grandparents. A quadroon has a biracial (mulatto) parent and one White parent. Octoroon means a person of fourth-generation Black ancestry. Genealogically, it means one-eighth Black. Typically an Octoroon has one great-grandparent who is of full African descent and seven great-grandparents who are not. Quintroon is a rarely used term that means a person of fifth-generation Black ancestry. A quintroon has one parent who is an octoroon and one White parent.

Many of these women, in pursuit of an improved life in White society, tried to hide their roots to pass as White, but often were discovered as being part Black and later punished by being forced back into a life of slavery. However, both enslaved and freeborn light-skinned Black women sometimes became the willing concubines of wealthy White southerners for the benefits of freedom and financial security. This system, called placage, involved a formal arrangement for White men to financially support Black women and their children in exchange for long-term sexual services. White men often met these women at "Quadroon Balls," a genteel sex market where sexual play often took place.

In many southern states, like Louisiana, Mississippi, Alabama and Florida, Quadroon Balls were very common. Taverns, opera houses, dance halls, theatres, and meeting places were often used to accommodate these mixed-race events. During the mid to late 1700s, White men were not expected to marry until their early thirties, and premarital sex with an intended White bride was inconceivable. As a result, many Black women soon became the concubines of White male colonists, who were sometimes the younger sons of noblemen, military men, plantation owners, merchants and administrators.

While this life provided a level of comfort and convenience for many Black women, it came with its set of challenges. These relationships were often temporary and provided no surety of permanent security. So, she often found herself exactly where she started, once again trying to bargain for her and her children's security. Furthermore, any discovery of her true identity by members of the larger society could result in her punishment. So the biracial woman's life was filled with both risk and reward.

WELFARE QUEEN

The welfare queen caricature is one of the more modern stereotypical depictions of Black women. The idea was conceptualized and brought to a national audience by Ronald Reagan in 1976, during his race for United States President. During the campaign, Reagan told the story of a Black woman from Chicago's South Side who was arrested for welfare fraud. In his own words, he said:

"She has 80 names, 30 addresses, 12 Social Security cards and is collecting veteran's benefits on four non-existing deceased husbands. And she is collecting Social Security on her cards. She's got Medicaid, getting food stamps, and she is collecting welfare under each of her names."

It was later discussed by Reagan that she made $150,000 from gaming welfare which afforded a nice house and a Cadillac. This newfound story created a media frenzy. Every news station tried to find this woman in order to put her on the evening news. Ironically, they never found her. Why? Reagan had made it up in order to push a political agenda during his campaign.

Though later proven to be fictitious, the idea stuck. Since Reagan never named a particular woman, the description soon became a widely accepted generalization of Black women. Soon after its inception, this false image took on a life of its own. While poor White women were given sympathy for their economic situation, Black women were criticized for their uncontrollable sexuality and excessive laziness.

Over time, the Welfare Queen came to be depicted as a lazy, uneducated, poor, un-wed, child-bearing Black woman who is living off the welfare system and milking government assistance for every penny she possibly can. She could have a job if she wanted to, but she prefers the benefits that come along with being a welfare queen: a hefty stipend, Medicaid, and food stamps. Because of her behavior, she is not admired by anyone, nor does she provoke sympathy. Further, because there is no man in the house, she is unable to properly supervise her delinquency-prone children who grow to become teenaged mothers, gang members, and other menaces to society.

She is a professional mother who will squeeze out a tribe of children for the sole purpose of reaping her most coveted reward: more government assistance. She's also known to supplement that government check with monies coming from all four fathers of her five illegitimate children. Rather than providing the necessities her family needs, she instead pampers herself with designer clothes, handbags, and other niceties that she could normally not afford.

Not only was this grossly exaggerated image created and widely accepted by the larger White society, it has further been perpetuated as well. One of the most recent cultural attacks comes from a White male comedian. The openly gay, White male Charles Knipp unapologetically plays a disturbingly stereotypical woman who goes by the name of 'Shirley Q Liquor.' Shirley is an African-American woman, who's also a "malt liquor guzzling welfare mother with nineteen kids, and drives a Caddy. Though Knipp's $70k-$90k a year one-man show income pales in comparison to the likes of Murphy, Perry and Lawrence, his portrayal is just as demeaning and damaging.

Ironically, there have been countless protests, organized movements and bans that have attempted to shut his performance completely down. However, these same protesters turn a blind eye to the ridicule and parodies of fat Black women when perpetuated by Black men. This speaks to our own cultural contradictions. When we do it (Black Folks), it's all in good, clean fun. When they do it (White Folks), it's an insensitive racist attack on our people. Unfortunately, this double standard has created a climate that has made it 'open-season' on all Black women.

This deeply penetrating image has unfairly associated the welfare system and government assistance with Blackness. A study on welfare stories in both print media and television news was conducted by Yale political scientist Martin Gilens. The print media analysis covered the 1960's through 1992. The TV analysis covered 1988-1994. The studies which were later published in 1996 and 1997, found the following:

- Sixty-two percent of poverty stories that appeared in TIME, Newsweek and U.S. News and World Report featured African-Americans.
- Sixty-five percent of network television news stories about welfare featured African-Americans.
- Fewer African-Americans are portrayed in "sympathetic" stories about poverty and welfare
- Newsmagazines depict almost 100 percent of the "underclass" as African-Americans.

These images then led people to the next conclusion: poor women choose to be on welfare because they fail to adhere to a set of core American values. Their apparent disregard for hard work, family values and sexual control has put them in this predicament.

Despite the skewed media depiction, this stereotype is historically incorrect. The welfare system was designed for poor White widows with children during the Great Depression. Blacks were excluded from the program on the grounds that they could find work in the fields or in other peoples' homes. Once Black women were able to benefit from welfare, it was met with great resistance because of the racist/sexist double standard in America which portrays poor White women as "down on their luck" and Black women as "sexually loose" who intentionally get pregnant in order to get more money from the state.

The Black Welfare Queen imagery is still alive and well today. Simply turn on the news, a television show, or movie and you will see how deeply entrenched this caricature is embedded in American folklore.

MATRIARCH (Strong Black Woman)

Why We Hate Black Women

The Matriarch stereotype is one of the main images regarding Black women that have been engrained in the minds of the American people. The Matriarch is a strong Black woman who has been forced to play dual roles as both mother and father to her children. For any number of reasons the father has either left the home and shirked all responsibility or is physically present but not living up to his duties. In essence, she is the head of the household and rules and dominates her family.

The Matriarch role is a hybrid caricature with a number of influences that can be found in the Mammy, the Welfare Queen and the Sapphire. Her physical appearance is similar to the exaggerated imagery of the mammy. She is depicted as dark, fat and ugly. Her posture, disposition and overall makeup are reminiscent of a man. In fact, from the 1950s to the 1990s the predominance of the Matriarch image took the place of the Mammy caricature while maintaining some similarity. However, there were some stark differences.

The Matriarch is the Mammy gone bad: a failed mammy. Unfortunately, she has spent too much time away from home working, has not properly supervised her children, is overly aggressive, and emasculates the men in her life. Like the Welfare Queen, she is the head of the household and poor, unable to bring up her children properly. Like the Sapphire she is overbearing, outspoken, and knows how to cut men down when necessary. However, she is not as mean or as womanly as the Sapphire. The Matriarch is also much less likely to have a man. If a man is present, he is often seen but not heard and usually takes a back seat to her authority.

The Matriarch imagery is depicted as a strong, unfeminine, domineering figure who is in all regards diametrically opposed to the idealized image of the typical White woman. White women have always been presented as docile, submissive, chaste and domesticated. Likewise, Black women have been burdened with the stigma of being matriarchal. While the term Matriarch is dated, the more contemporary label for this type of woman would be the 'Strong Black Woman'.

The notion of the Strong Black Woman has saturated the Black American landscape for the past 60 years. The tag line message 'strong, Black and independent' has reverberated within the African American oral tradition so much so, that it has placed Black women in a one-dimensional role with no possible means of escape. This particular identity has been so engrained within the Black adolescent female mind that any resistance to this social construct would be a denial of one's race and gender. In other words, there's no such thing as a weak Black woman.

Not only has White-controlled Hollywood displayed this image, but the Black community has overwhelmingly accepted this role as a reality as well. It has been expressed in our movies, our music, our literature, our social and religious institutions, our mother-daughter conversations, and our overall cultural experience. It is the most embraced and celebrated stereotype of them all. An extensive analysis of this role is provided in the chapter *Too Strong For Your Own Good.*

Conclusion

The Black female experience in America is a peculiar one. The African-American woman has always been the racial and sexual 'Other' in a predominately White society. Throughout history White men have created a multitude of one-dimensional, fictitious depictions of Black women. Interestingly, each caricature was well thought out and planned, and had a specific intent in mind. Whether it was for wealth accumulation, sexual exploitation or cultural degradation, they have succeeded in the deconstruction of the Black Female image and perception.

To add insult to injury, the mantle (or baton) of racial/gender inequality has been passed from White men to Black men. From Hollywood to Hip Hop, many Black men have embraced the role of 'Master' and have perpetuated the stereotypical imagery of Black women which still exists today. While White men exploited Black women on the auction block for financial gain and sexual exploration, many Black men follow in the same tradition. Though

Why We Hate Black Women

Black women continue to be marginalized as angry, strong, and independent, much of their fascination rests in their role as strippers on modern day auction blocks: strip club table-tops which is often depicted in Hip Hop music videos.

Three hundred and ninety years since the inception of slavery in America, Black women continue to struggle with plantation-rooted stereotypes that have negatively affected their work, relationships, and overall personal happiness. They continue to remain trapped in a false reality that has placed many limitations on the lives of Black women.

In order to begin to solve this problem, Black women must collectively redefine themselves and challenge the existing stereotypes that have become mainstream in American society. Audre Lorde said, "If we do not define ourselves for ourselves, we will be defined by others for their use and to our detriment."

The Tale About Black Tail

The Black female body is envied by some, desired
by most and devalued by all.
~Hasani Pettiford

*I*t appears that Black women in America have been reduced to nothing more than a piece of Black tail. Whether one has risen to the heights of an Oprah Winfrey or another has graced the cover of a Black men's magazine, their value has been made parallel. While African-Americans have culturally celebrated the aesthetics of a 'Big 'Ole Butt', it has historically represented savage sexuality and racial inferiority in the eyes of the larger majority.

Despite the world's paradoxical obsession with the unique physique of Black women, little to no value has been placed on their beauty. In fact, a Black woman's backside has often trumped all other qualities that define her worth. Unfortunately, women have often been observed through a sexual lens and less focus has been placed on their moral character, educational accomplishments and occupational pursuits. Just consider our First Lady Michelle Obama.

During the 2008 election campaign both Black and White press seemed to have a strange obsession with Michelle Obama's backside. One Black feminist blogger wrote "Good God, she's got a butt...Obama's baby (mama) got back." An African-American online forum was quoted as saying "OMG, her butt is humongous!" Others have described it as a 'solid, round, black, class-A boo-tay'.

Salon.com published an article by an African-American writer entitled *First Lady Got Back.* The article explained, "While Barack sought to calm the waters with speeches about unity and commonality, Michelle's body was sending a different message: the one clear signifier of her blackness that couldn't be tamed, muted or made invisible was her big ole' butt."

Meanwhile, *The Daily Show* featured an elderly Jewish couple from a Florida political focus group who disapprovingly described Michelle as a "horse" with a big "tuchis." The husband went on to say "all of them (meaning Black women) are built that way." Not only does the 'White gaze' see the shape of her Black backside as abnormal, it perceives her as animalistic. To further the point, one blogger called her King Kong's sister.

All of these comments have played a part in depreciating the value of her accomplishments as a wife, mother and career woman by focusing on Mrs. Obama's physical attributes. In essence, she's been denied a certain level of respect that would normally be offered to any other woman in her position. Whether the comments were made in admiration or with pure disgust, the outcome remains the same: First Lady Michelle Obama, along with countless Black women in this society, has been reduced to nothing more than a piece of Black tail.

Interestingly, the public and private discussion of the Black female body is nothing new. Our discussion of this topic must be informed by the long history of sexual exploitation Black women have endured. When African women arrived on the shores of America with their voluptuous bodies, a stark contrast to the figures of European women, it was assumed that they were savage beasts without sexual inhibitions. European men immediately saw opportunity in the exploitation of these women. In fact, the bodies of Black women have had a long standing history of being used as a product for European consumption. The tradition of exhibiting Black women in Western societies dates all the way back to Christopher Columbus. In 1492, he brought several Arawaks from the New World to Queen Isabella's court in Spain, where one of them remained on display for two years. Exhibiting Black female bodies as a popular practice reached its height in the nineteenth century

in both Europe and the United States when freak shows became fairly popular.

The exhibition of Black women for public entertainment in circuses, zoos, and museums became a profitable industry at the time. In fact, popular traveling shows like Buffalo Bill's Wild West Show and Barnum and Bailey's Circus were known for their human displays. With desires that could not be satiated with humiliating displays of living Black women, White men also publicly exhibited the dissected and embalmed remains of Black female bodies, particularly the skulls and sexual organs.

Trophy heads, body parts, and other skeletal remains still reside in the collections of many Western museums; this fact strongly suggests that European fascination with exhibiting Black bodies is not a phenomenon of the distant past but a reality of the present as well. While history could provide us with innumerable examples, one woman has epitomized Black female sexual exploitation.

Sarah Baartman "The Black Hottentot Venus"

Saartjie "Sarah" Baartman, commonly known as Hottentot Venus was born in South Africa in 1789. Her indigenous name is uncertain, but the name Saartjie is Dutch for "Little Sara." The Khoi Khoi tribe, which she originates from, were derogatorily referred to as "Hottentots," *(one of inferior culture and intellect)*.

They were considered the lowest, most savage types of human beings. This assessment of their humanity later became a justification for their targeted extermination and removal. During a routine extermination raid by the Dutch, Baartman lost her husband and family and eventually migrated to the urban center of Cape Town for survival.

Saartjie Baartman belonged to a people whose women possessed a strikingly peculiar body type. Khoisan women projected a behind similar to a right-angled triangle, nearly horizontal with a 45 degree slope. More of their body fat was stored in the buttocks rather than in the thighs and belly. They also possessed elongated labia minora (the fold of skin from the clitoris) that would hang as far as three to four inches below the vagina. The combination of Baartman's oversized buttocks, genitals and breasts triggered her slave master's brother to insist that she travel abroad to display herself before the world in exchange for fortune.

In the most degrading display, Baartman was kept in a cage under the constant threat of violence and exhibited like a wild beast. She was made to parade naked along a slightly elevated platform. She was often obligated to walk, stand or sit at her keeper's orders, and told to show off her large genitals, which varied in their appearance from those of Europeans. Onlookers were even allowed to touch her genitals for an additional fee. This dehumanizing display extended beyond the confines of a circus. The show was also featured in museums, bars and universities all throughout Europe.

Baartman's popularity attracted the attention of scientists and quickly became the object of scientific and medical research. Once the Baartman peep show lost its steam, she was forced to prostitute her body for profit. Shortly after her transition from forced pornography to prostitution, she died in Paris at the young age of 26 years old due to physical complications that remain unclear. But even in death her body wasn't allowed to rest.

Her body was taken and copied in a plaster-cast and then dissected, leaving her skeleton, pickled brain and her pickled genitalia preserved in jars of formaldehyde for display in Paris museums up until 1985. White scientists and other onlookers interpreted her body as morbid and animalistic. Her vagina was compared to an ape and the size of her genitalia was considered proof of her insatiable desire for sex.

Due to world-wide mounting pressure, the French were forced to remove the entire display from public view and to store the display out of sight. In 1995, the South African government fought for the return of Baartman's remains and began a nearly decade-long fight with the French government over this disturbing history. After seven long years, in March 2002, the French Senate finally agreed to return Baartman's remains, including her preserved organs, for burial in her homeland after 187 years of captivity.

Though Baartman was not the first African woman to parade through the streets of Europe under the auspices of European rule, she certainly was the most memorable. As she left her native land of South Africa, she never knew that she would become the icon of racial inferiority and Black female sexuality for the next 175 years.

The Black Venus Lives On

The tale about Black tail still persists today. Even though Saartjie "Sarah" Baartman's remains have been put to rest, the unfortunate legacy of the Black 'Hottentot Venus' remains. The stereotypical imagery of Black women, which was created by European men, has been perpetuated by Black men and embraced by many Black women. So, the spirit of Black Venus continues to dwell among us today.

Turn to BET (Black Entertainment Television) after ten o'clock on any given evening and you will see model, actress and Hip Hop video vixen Buffie Carruth aka "Buffie the Body" sport a 36-24-45 frame as she entices viewers to call in and talk with all of her 40 inch plus behind girlfriends. Although, late-night cable commercials flaunt tight shots of her breasts, eyes, flowing hair and her famous buttocks, she claims that her modeling is about more than the money and fame. She boasts that she's using the opportunity to be a role model and help change stereotypes. Buffie actually believes her work is empowering to Black women.

What Buffie Carruth doesn't understand is that the very existence of her alter-ego Buffie the Body is the fulfillment of a stereotype that has been around for over two hundred years. A Black woman who submits to behaving according to this stereotype may not be forced to walk, bend over and exhibit her parts before European men within a circus or a traveling show but

71

she voluntarily performs p-poppin and booty clappin' dances in front of Black men in clubs and on music video sets all across this country. She may not be on display within the exhibits of European museums; however, she's plastered all over magazine spreads, posters, MySpace pages, websites and videos.

Buffie proudly proclaims, "I'm the definition of a true Black woman." But, most women with behinds as big as Buffie's don't have the measurements of 36-24-45. In fact, most women with a size 45 behind have stomachs and thighs of equal proportion to go along with it. But Buffie is not the only one vying for the top spot of the most bodacious.

Magazines like *XXL, King, Smooth Girl, The Source, Black Men's Magazine* and several others feature scantily-clad women, often complete with an interview of the featured model. The subjects of these shoots range from professional models to well-known musicians and actresses. These magazines typically reject the "stick-figured" women used as models in other men's magazines, and instead promote the buxom and curvaceous figures of their own models.

Reality-based television star Chandra Davis a.k.a. London Charles/Deelishis from VH-1's hit TV show *Flavor of Love* is among the ranking of women with big butts. The combination of her reality show finalist status and her 36-27-42 frame paved the way for a life of instant urban stardom. You also have models, video vixens and porn stars like Melyssa Ford, Toccara Jones, Angel Lola Luv, Ice La Fox, and a host of other women displayed on television and magazine covers.

While big breasts are the major focal point of most White men's magazines, big butts are the focus of most Black men's magazines. Many of these women have made a successful career of flaunting their bodies for compensation. One of the main arenas that Black Tail is highly exposed in is the Hip Hop industry.

Hip Hop Booty Addiction

The Hip Hop music industry has unapologetically carried the torch and fulfilled the legacy of Sarah Baartman. The merger of music and Black beauty on display is no new phenomenon. This lucrative combination has been around since the days of Slick Rick, Dana Dane and Doug E.Fresh. However, what was once clever has now become raunchy and over-the-top. Black women with large derrieres have always existed, but the Hip Hop industry has presented it as the only visual expression of beauty. In fact, there is an unhealthy fixation on the 'Black booty.'

There is a long history of sexuality within Hip Hop music and the Black butt has been the central theme of much of its visual and verbal message. Whether we're talking about Sir Mix-A-Lot's *Baby Got Back*, Tribe Called Quest's *Bonita Apple Bum*, Juvenile's *Back That Thang Up*, R. Kelly's *Feelin' On Your Booty*, Black-Eyed Peas' *My Hump*, D4L's *Laffy Taffy*, Bubba Sparxxx's *Ms. New Booty*, Ludacris' *P-Poppin* or Nelly's *Tip Drill*, the videos tend to get more explicit with each new song.

The large Black butt comes along with certain assumptions. It has been associated with a woman's promiscuousness, sexual talent, high appetite for sex and easy entry. This representation was clearly demonstrated in Nelly's controversial *Tip Drill* video. This music video makes it hard to determine what is worse: the imagery or the message.

It is a seven minute pornographic display of countless Black women p-poppin' and booty clappin' while poolside at an Atlanta mansion. Additionally, there are bathroom tub scenes of half naked women performing simulated sex on each another. Meanwhile, the Black men make it rain as they drop, stuff and force money inside the crotch and cleavage of several women. As disrespectful as the imagery is, the meaning of *Tip Drill* is just as bad.

Most interpret the phrase tip drill to mean a female with a nice body but an ugly face due to the lyrics "it must be yo a-- 'cause it ain't yo face, I need a tip drill, I need a tip drill." Nelly is implying that is he attracted to a girl solely due to her buttocks. The reason these girls are referred to as tip drills is because they have large buttocks, which is ideal for a sexual activity known as tip drilling which involves placing the penis between the buttocks with/without penetration. The term can also be used as a verb to describe the repetitive screwing-like motion (grind 'n bounce) of a woman engaging in sex, and as a noun to describe either the man or woman involved in this simulated sex act.

Other interpretations of the term suggest that a guy would rather hit it from the back because of the magnitude of her behind and the wish to avoid looking at her face. Just consider the following lyrics "toot that a-- up mama put that dip in ya back and let me tip drill just let me tip drill." And if it could get no worse, Nelly brags that a true tip drill must be down for engaging in sex with a brutha' and all of his boys as well. The lyrics read, "I said it ain't no fun unless we all get some, I need a tip drill, we need a tip drill."

But the video wouldn't be complete without video vixen Whyte Chocolate bent over and spread eagle as Nelly swipes a credit card straight down the crack of her behind. Wow Nelly, way to go! That split second procedure sent a message throughout the world that a Black woman's worth and value is connected to the size, shape and accessibility of her behind (or overall body). While the women in the video gained a nominal monetary compensation for the use of their bodies, Nelly raked in a truck load of cash.

Not only is Nelly a multi-platinum recording artist/superstar, he is a fashion designer who has created an urban fashion clothing line to clothe his greatest obsession; Black women's behinds. His Apple Bottoms line caters to females of all shapes and sizes who want to "liberate the natural curves of a woman's body." His signature logo is the apple, which resembles the area of the body Nelly believes all women should be proud of. His success has led to a full clothing line for women containing jeans, skirts, shorts, shirts, and even jackets.

As a lover of the best that Hip Hop has to offer, I don't mean to attack Nelly; however, we can no longer allow our love for Hip Hop to blindside us to the reality of what is taking place. Nelly is not alone. Other rappers, DJs, corporate executives and the women who voluntarily exploit themselves are to be questioned. At the end of the day, this 'Booty Addiction' has contributed to the craze that both men and women have for a big butt. Unfortunately, the desire to obtain Black Tail has led many down a wayward path.

In Search For More Tail

Countless young Black women spend their precious time trying to achieve a video vixen figure in order to feel better about themselves and appeal to Black men. Even models and strippers who work in the entertainment industry admittedly reveal they were not born with big butts. They built them. The plump and fat booty with hips and thighs shaped like a coke bottle have become standard within the industry because of techniques that have remained a secret among sex workers. This coveted secret that directly sends fat below the waistline has been sought out by ordinary sistahs in the community.

Unfortunately, the media, music videos and peers have placed added pressure and insecurities in the minds of women and have told them that they must have a big butt in order to achieve status, success, financial independence, and most importantly, to secure a man. Thus, children grow up with the same insecurities as adults. As a result, strippers and video vixens, who were once looked down upon because of their lewd and exploitive behavior, have become the prototype of beauty among many Black girls.

Beyond porn star secrets, Black women are resorting to exercises, butt implants, enlargement injections, Brazilian butt lifts, pills, potions and lotions in order to obtain the symbol of Black womanhood: the booty. Black women from Jamaica, Haiti and America's southern states, where large populations of Caribbeans reside, are known for ingesting 'Fowl Pills' to obtain a bigger rear-end. These are pills used by farmers to fatten farm animals, particularly chickens.

Many Black women in the United States who desire a bigger, rounder and fuller butt are stashing away cash to get 'Butt Surgery'. But not all medical procedures are made the same. While some can afford to go to licensed medical physicians to get gluteoplasty (butt augmentation surgery), others are settling for the more affordable butt injections.

Though medical procedures can cost upwards of $15,000 to $20,000, many are opting for the 'ghetto hook up'. For a price of $500 to $3,000 many women are opting for the illegal and potentially lethal cosmetic treatment. Unlicensed buttpreneurs are traveling across the country conducting 'Butt Pumping Parties' within hotel rooms and private homes with a gallon jug of silicone in one hand and a fist full of syringes in the other offering to inject women with 'Hydrogel'.

Hydrogel is a liquid-based substance made up of 95% water and 5% polyacrylamide and is typically used as skin filler for wrinkles and depressed scars. Unfortunately, many women aren't getting Hydrogel pumped into their bodies. Instead, these Hydrogel promoters use over-the-counter industrial-grade silicone purchased in hardware stores which are typically used as sealant to help close small openings that are difficult to shut with other materials such as concrete or drywall. This substance is known for having toxic contaminants.

This foreign substance is injected into the body and then seeps into the bloodstream, nerves and organs. It isn't sterile and may cause infections all throughout the body. While some leave the surgery table with no complications, others have been known to have severe cases of vomiting, back pain, diarrhea, muscle deterioration, extreme weight loss, blood clots, failed kidneys and lungs, and possibly even death.

With all that said, so many women want to continue with the procedure in hopes of finally obtaining a big 'ole butt. There are countless women who suffer from insecurities because of the shape of their bodies. A question from a suffering spouse was recently posted on my website. She felt inadequate because her husband desired something that she could not offer. She became a victim of the butt craze. She writes:

Chapter 4: The Tale About Black Tail

I am painfully hurt by my husband's admission that he is not and never really was sexually attracted to me as much as he could be if I were a woman with a big behind. Our black culture dictates that I must now have a big behind to be considered attractive.

By most standards I am attractive and smart. My husband, otherwise, says I am a good wife and he loves me. We barely make love and his favorite sites are sites of women with big behinds. I am envious and jealous I admit. Not really because of their big butts but because he greatly desires what I don't have. Faithful to my marriage I feel that I have no recourse.

I am currently working out and am in decent shape. We do not want to divorce, but I always feel like he's looking on the other side of the fence. The reality is that he wants what I don't have. How do I handle this? I am slowly healing from the obsession of it all and his lack of sexual interest in me.

He says he's always felt this way but tried not to be shallow. My pain seems unbearable at times. What do you suggest? I am currently working on getting a "butt job" done just to hopefully be able to fulfill his "needs" as a wife. Intellectually, I know he sounds like a shallow person and I could make the argument that my butt should not define my sex relationship with my hubby but reality says otherwise...This has put a strain on our sex life and he thinks I'm overreacting, which makes me suspicious because he seems to accept it too easily. Why is it this way? Why aren't brains and beauty enough? There is no worse feeling than being with someone who doesn't want you sexually.

Unfortunately, this Black woman is not alone. Many married women are suffering in their marriage because of physical incompatibility and the obsession with big butts promoted in society and the media. Single women are affected by the butt craze as well. One 23 year-old Californian girl said *"I'm not looking for a white girl big booty, I want a ghetto booty, too big for my body booty. Is that possible?"*

Another sistah out of Florida said, *"I just want some booty. It doesn't have to be a big ghetto stripper booty with a mind of its own, but it would be nice to not be the only female in my family with no butt. I just feel left out!"*

One 32-year old single Philadelphian woman who responded to my online blog said:

"In the fight against European standards of beauty the 'Butt' has been in the forefront. Black women are associated (and self proclaimed) to have large hips, large lips and thick thighs. These are cultural aesthetics that we pride ourselves on. It's hard when you do not possess these features, you feel disconnected from a cultural heritage...and inheritance. Women who grow up in a family with long hair learn to desire hair, women whose family is slim want to be thinner and if you are surrounded by women in your family who are shapely you want to be shapely. It's no different than weaves and push up bras.

If the white standard of beauty is flat with long hair and the black standard of beauty is butt and hips, what happens if you don't fit either? Yes everyone should love themselves for who and what they are but asking this of an individual is a lot, especially when these desires are initiated in childhood. Women need to become more accepting of each other and stop competing and hating on each other, allowing men to divide us and have pick of the litter (so to speak). Personally, there are features and traits I love about myself but I would like a Butt...a big one because from everything I see I'm supposed to have one."

After reading these women's responses you would think that being a sistah without a booty is a handicap. That somehow they're less of a woman. This thinking has affected many women's self-esteem and overall perception of themselves. While the quest for a bigger butt may offer a form of satisfaction, it is no guarantee of one's overall happiness.

Chapter 5

Hatred In The Name of Hip Hop

"Women are treated 'merely as a hole to be filled by men, and the songs have hundreds of disparaging [insulting] remarks."
~Unknown

For a little over 30 years, Hip Hop music has been a part of America's pastime. Over time, it's become more than just a genre of music it has become an American subculture that flexes its muscles on an international stage. It has been said that if you take away Hip Hop, you'd take away the voice of a generation of Black youth and young adults. It's been one of the only venues where youth can verbally spit and truly be themselves.

Hip Hop is a genre of music seen as a cultural vehicle for self-expression and social reflection of the community. However, there is a war for the soul going on within the Hip Hop nation. An overwhelmingly large segment of Hip Hop music has transformed into a sample-heavy, highly materialistic, sexually vulgar, cultural phenomenon that is far removed from its earlier social/political activism. Much of mass distributed Hip Hop is now materialistic, hedonistic, misogynistic, shallow and violent.

If you're thinking I'm being too critical just consider the lyrics. Some artists have gone from raunchy to downright ridiculous. Rapper DMX spits from the heart in his song *X is Coming* with the following lyrics, "If you got a daughter older than fifteen, I'mma rape her." In another song he refers to several women as "dirty b-tches" and "rats," as in hood rats, with whom he had sex on project rooftops, in stairwells, and in parks.

Atlanta-based artist Ludacris delivers instructions in his song *P-Poppin*: "Now pop that coochie, you know the procedure. If you want this cash gotta make that a—shake like a seizure." Artist Joe Budden in the remix of Usher's *Confessions* says "If she's talkin' bout keepin' it/ one hit to the stomach, she's leakin' it." So rape, pulling trains, forced abortions, prostitution and physical violence details the young Black woman's experience on wax (or CD).

Hip Hop music is the only art-form where you can call Black women a B-tch, Ho, Trick, Slut, Freak, Tramp, Hoochie, Gold Digger, Skeezer, Woo-Wop, Flip-Flop, Flipper, Bird, Chicken Head, Slore, Cunt, Tip Drill, Butta Head, Smut, Noodle, Scank, Jawn, Hood Rat, Shorty, Wifey, Heifer, Bust It Baby, Track Star, Runner, Jump Off, Slut Box, Cum Bucket, Scally Wag, Cranker, Brick House, Bobble Head, Rolla, Strocker and every other degrading word that an artist can think of in his lyrics, and parade her around in front of everyone on a stripper's pole while people applaud with pride.

Not only do these artists advocate sexually conquering Black women, they verbally encourage prostituting and beating them anytime they so called 'get out of pocket.' So, from the lyrics on the radio to the videos on the tube, rappers engage in misogynistic behavior towards Black women. In its simplest form, a lot of the music is verbal assault wrapped up in a tight beat and catchy hook.

The *Black's Law Dictionary* defines sexual assault as "Any willful attempt or threat to inflict injury upon the person of another, when coupled with an apparent present ability so to do, and any intentional display of force such as would give the victim reason to fear or expect immediate bodily harm, constitutes an assault. An assault may be committed without actually or striking, or doing bodily harm, to the person of another." (p. 114)

As clearly stated, assault doesn't need actual physical contact to be considered assault. The threat of violence is all that is needed to constitute an act of assault. Unfortunately, much of Hip Hop music can easily be placed within this definition.

Author Pearl Cleage clearly explained in her book *Mad at Miles*, the socialization process that has taught society to accept the dehumanization of Black women. She writes,

"It is impossible to live in America and not be tainted by sexism and a participant in it, either as a victim or a perpetrator. As women, by the end of our African American girlhoods, we have learned and perfected a dizzying variety of slave behaviors which we are rewarded for mastering by the men who made them up in the first place.

As men, they were taught that we were inferior, unworthy of their respect, subject to their whim and present on earth primarily for their sexual pleasure and the bearing and mothering of their children. We were all taught that it is acceptable for them to hit us when they think we have "asked for it" and that their opinions carry more weight in all critical decisions simply because they were men and therefore assumed to be of superior knowledge and more vast experience." (p. 41)

This dark reality expressed in Cleage's book continues to remain apparent within our music today. As long as misogyny remains the message of choice, the pimp life will always remain at the forefront of Hip Hop music and culture. And this male-dominated culture has restricted the roles women are allowed to play. While some have remained true to who they are, countless others have willingly fallen in line.

Black Women's Role In Hip Hop

At present, Black males continue to move up through the ranks of Hip Hop leaving very little room for Black women. As a result, the women who embrace this lifestyle are left with very few choices as to what roles they are allowed to play if they want to be in the game. Actually, there are few roles open to women who want to be a major part of Hip Hop. Essentially, there are few female rappers left. The top of the heap belongs to the males, and the women who want to immerse themselves in this culture must acquiesce to a limited selection of demeaning roles. There are five major categories in which Black women can play a part in Hip Hop.

Rappers

The Black female rapper has become somewhat of an endangered species. Long gone are the days of Queen Latifah, MC Lyte, and Lauryn Hill. In fact, the last time the Grammy Awards had a 'Best Female Rap Category' was in 1993. With an art form that continues to maintain a strong male presence, many female rappers have taken on the 'B-tch' stigma in order to sell albums. With a message that portrays a lifestyle of sex, drugs, money and rough street life, artists like Rah Digga, Mia X, Sole, Mocha, Trina and Da Brat have conveyed a message that has been deemed disparaging to Black womanhood.

Since its inception, Hip Hop has always been a male dominated environment and many women have been almost forced to accept the b-tch stigma: a sexually hot and bothered, ill-tempered, malicious female. *Essence Magazine* writer Joan Morgan wrote, *The Bad Girls of Hip Hop*, and stated that "sex has become the bartering chip many women use to gain protection, wealth, and power."

Entering an industry where millions have been made by pimpin' poontang, too many female rappers have sold out for money by embracing the sex-me message. Rather than Hip Hop being used as a vehicle to empower, several female artists have written artificial rhymes that welcome hittin' the jackpot between their legs. This sexualized style of rap gets progressively worse because artists discover that in order to titillate a sexually overindulged society they have to be a bit more bold and edgy than the last female.

However, no one has proven to be more sexually outrageous than Hip Hop's nasty girls Lil' Kim and Foxy Brown. They have both exuded the ghetto glamgirl image, spewing raunchy pornographic and materialistic lyrics. Flaunting her blonde hair, blue eyes and silicone breasts, some Hip-Hop fans have argued that Lil' Kim has gone from rap queen to drag queen. Similarly, it has been said when Foxy Brown takes off all her make-up she looks like Doo-Doo Brown.

Years spent rivaling for the number one Diva Ho spot, both Lil' Kim and Foxy Brown competed with one another to see who would take off the most clothing without showing every nook and cranny. While Foxy posed for *Vibe* magazine's cover grabbing her breasts and crotch, Lil' Kim attempted to top her efforts by wearing nothing but a hat and boots in a photo shoot for her second album. Lil' Kim declares "Sex is power; b--tches do what they have to do to get paid." In the same breath she states "I represent all the females." This is truly problematic.

Meanwhile *The Source* stated that Foxy's second album "*Chyna Doll* was important because it provides a roadmap through the mind of a Black girl..." This is truly a scary statement. With very explicit messages saturating radio airwaves across the nation, many have argued that these two artists have transformed more and more young female listeners into nymphomaniac, foul-mouthed, ill-tempered, malicious little girls.

Foxy Brown admitted in the February edition of *Rap Pages*: "I'm not a role model, as far as what I say on my records. I say things that a role model just should not say. My fans just see Foxy and how it is out there. But that's not me. Foxy is just a character I become when I am out. At home I'm not like this at all. I am in my sweats and I am just chilling." Unfortunately, her admittance to a sex gimmick for mere entertainment is not enough to repair the damage. Too many young Black girls have already had their innocence taken, their minds shattered and their lives destroyed.

Why We Hate Black Women

The following are lyrics recited by Hip Hop artists that have a sexual influence over their listeners.

"I'm the baddest b---h, you gotta admit that,
69 ways, you know I'm wit that,
And I'mma shake my money maker,
I'mma shake this thing like a salt shaker,
Cause ain't nothin' wrong wit the bump and grind,
When I do this thing up jump behind,
I ride like a choo choo train,
Little mama, I'm fittin' to do this thing.
Front, back, side to side,
That's how you slip and slide
What's up little daddy, trick a fat stack
Representin' for my girls wit a fat back."
Trina   'Pull Over (That A#$ Too Fat)'

What would you do if your son was at home,
cryin' all alone on the bedroom floor cause he's hungry?
And the only way to feed him is to sleep
with a man for a little bit of money,
and his daddy's gone; somewhere smokin' rock now,
in and out of lock down,
I ain't got a job now. So for you, this is just a good time,
but for me this is what I call life.
City High   'What Would You Do?'

Nuttin' make a woman feel betta than Berrettas and
Amarettas,
butta leathers and mad cheddaz.
Chillin in a Benz with my ami-gos,
Tryin to stick a nigga for his pe-sos.
If you say so, then I'm the same chick that you wanna get with,
lick up in my twat.

Gotta hit the spot,
If not don't test the poom poom nanny nanny, donny, heyyy!!!
Lil' Kim _'No Time'_

Aint no nigga like the one I got,
sleeps around but he gives me a lot.
Foxy Brown _'My Life'_

What's discouraging is that many of these artists think their message is truly empowering - that somehow being sexually uninhibited and materialistic is a step in the right direction for Black women. While Lil' Kim prides herself as being a self-proclaimed feminist, she admits to charging men for the pooh-nanny while seeking loving relationships.

Typically, mainstream female rappers, today, are left with only two choices: 1) they can become clones of their male counterparts, taking on the hard-core masculine image of brute dominance, or, 2) they can subjugate themselves into the over-sexed, porn role. The reality of the situation is that to succeed today as a female rapper, you must morph yourself into one of these two categories. And once you have, you are stuck with it. There is NO going back. So, in effect, these women, in order to play in the game, have become the very thing they profess to hate.

As mentioned above, the saddest part is that these women are looked up to by our youth, especially young Black females. Despite Foxy Brown's assertion that she's not a role model, and that she's just playing the part, the fact is that fans are fans, and tend to idolize and imitate what they see their "heroes" doing.

Just consider VH1's ego-trip _Miss Rap Supreme_. It is an atrocious display of Black and White female artists competing for the crown of best female rapper. Except for a few who expressed creativity and strong lyrical flow, most voluntarily placed themselves in the role of a hard-core b-tch (who will quickly stab

85

any nigga who looks at them the wrong way) or a slutty b-tch (who will crack their legs open at the drop of a hat). What they haven't grasped is that being sexy or strong doesn't mean being nasty or hyper-masculine.

Unfortunately, positive female rappers aren't known. They can't seem to get record deals, mass marketing, or distribution. Why? Record labels, corporate executives, and a host of other individuals including many Hip Hop fans have decided that there is no market for them. Therefore, they remain invisible and the gap remains wide open.

Video Hotties

Pick any current video by an A-List Hip-Hop artist, and what you'll see is a bevy of scantily clad women being taken advantage of in the name of entertainment. However, video girls still line up to drop it like it's hot. These women enter Hip Hop by denigrating themselves and allowing themselves to be used. In an effort to gain recognition and status, they accept treatment and behavior that they would not tolerate on the street from strangers. They give themselves over to the wills, whims and desires of the video producer and artist.

It all begins at the casting session where the women show off their assets. They know that sex sells so they come in dressed very seductive. In fact, before many of them hit the set they're told to wear something tight and sexy in order to show legs, butts and breasts on demand. And many will do it without hesitation because they are looking to score their first video.

The typical casting call routine fosters the sexploitation experienced on a set. Girls from across the country show up and get a number. They wait in line for hours to take a snap shot. Often they're required to dance in front of a camera. Some girls believe that in order for them to get the role, they have to flash more than a smile. They will take their shirt off and attempt to seduce the director with their breasts. They'll drop something on the floor and seductively bend over to pick it up while exposing their g-string panties or bare bottom.

Once selected, some women are chosen as principal models and receive maximum exposure time. Others are selected as extras to create the atmosphere for the video. While principal models get star treatment, and upwards of $1500 a day, the extras make a measly $150 before taxes. The social pecking order on the set creates a high level of competition which encourages some women to go the extra mile just to get noticed. Women might wear less clothes or dance in a way to get more camera time. But those who aren't willing to go along with the program are often left out. Women who are uncomfortable joining an army of voluptuous, thonged and bikinied women can find themselves at odds with the casting directors and can be ill placed on the set or sent home.

With a vast array of girls on a video set waiting to perform, time can often creep by. For instance, there may only be a half an hour of camera time during a 10 hour day. So, to fill the time, a party may ensue. A room full of girls, male crew members, artists and members of his entourage will dance, drink and get loose. Inappropriate behavior may soon follow. Girls get hit on. Workers on the set may ask the girls for sex or sexual play. Artists will ask to sleep with models. Often, if a woman turns down advances her job could be on the line. Some are even told "I want to sleep with you and based on your answer, that's how far you're gonna get." One director on a video set boldly cornered a girl and whipped his penis out in anticipation of an erotic exchange.

Low totem pole crew members who get a title like director assistant will use that with a girl in order to get sex. Depending on how eager she may be, a girl will look at him as the only thing standing in between her and fame. Sometimes the worst offenders are not the directors or artists but their boys. The artist's entourage is often a girl's worst nightmare. They display disgusting behavior, cat call, hiss and even grab body parts. Some girls who can't get next to the artist will settle for the entourage.

87

Strippers

The other class of women you'll see in Hip Hop is comprised of strippers. Though they may be beautiful in appearance, they are not the models selected to grace the camera as a possible on-air romantic personality. Rather, these women are hand-picked from local strip clubs to offer a sexual dance performance to titillate its viewers. They shake, pop, gyrate, swing from poles, bend over, spread their charms, take it from behind and get busy with both men and women while on set.

They are often seen in videos being hauled around by guys like pieces of meat. Their legs are pulled apart while their crotches and behinds are shoved toward the camera. While all of this is being done, they meticulously keep a smile on their face while champagne and crisp twenty, fifty and one hundred dollar bills land on their female flesh. As humiliating and denigrating as this may be, they still seem to be drawn to the allure of fame and fortune.

Far away from the rented yachts and shiny Bentleys, they perform in a much more down and dirty type of Hip Hop video. These uncensored videos were of the type shown on the T&A fest known as 'Uncut.' Uncut was a program that played videos late night on BET before it was pulled for being too raunchy. The videos were sold on DVDs and made tons of money. And everyone's doing it. Ludacris' *P-Poppin* video and Nelly's *Tip Drill* video are the most recognizable examples of the new pornographic-styled video. These video sets often do not require casting calls because girls are hired through a local strip club as well as other venues.

As you watch these soft-pornographic videos, nothing is left up to the imagination. These mini-movies exhibit blurred out genital shots, booty clappin' and p-ssy poppin' contests, flesh jiggling, breast cleavage, butt cleavage, crotch shots, a display of sexual acrobatic techniques, pole dancing, and women tonguing and sexually riding each other in bathroom scenes.

As lewd as this may be, the stripper craze is not a new phenomenon. The celebration of strip club culture, booty music, and the "Dirty South" mantra began in the south in the late 1980s and early 1990s. Acts like 2 Live Crew helped set the stage for 'Crunk,' a southern offshoot of Hip Hop, which has merged strip club culture with Hip Hop music to create what some critics refer to as 'Strip-Hop'.

We certainly live in an era of the "stripper chick." In fact, the strip club has become one of the primary venues for Hip Hop enterprise. New music releases are now tested in strip clubs before they hit the airways. According to *Billboard* -- "it's no longer just the hardworking women who make money at strip clubs. These late-night hangouts, with their booming sound systems and gender-mixed crowds, have become big business for the record industry, particularly for Hip Hop labels. The music industry increasingly has embraced the strip club out of necessity and convenience."

Jermaine Dupri, president of urban music for Virgin Records says, "Strip clubs have become the main breaking place for records, especially in the South." The strip club and Hip Hop culture have merged two multi-billion dollar industries together which in turn have delivered a swift blow against the humanity of Black women. The VH1-sponsored documentaries, "*Hip-Hop and Hot Sex*", and "*Hip-Hop Videos and Sexploitation on the Set*", were created from the fusion of Hip Hop and the stripper/porn industry.

The mainstreaming of 'Strip Hop' has led artists beyond the scope of music videos. Hip Hop's porn-focused crossover movement has produced Mystikal's *Liquid City*, Snoop Dogg's *Buckwild Bus Tour*, *Doggystyle*, and *Diary of a Pimp*, G-Unit's *Groupie Love*, Luther "Uncle Luke" Campbell's *Best of Luke's Freakshows, Volumes 1-6*, and Lil' Jon and the Eastside Boyz's *American Sex Series*. With the profit and popularity that artists gain from producing these docu-films, there seems to be no clear end in sight. So, the fortune and fame of these artists are solely dependent upon the sexual labor of Black women.

Groupies

The female groupie is nothing more than a celebrity-seeker. She has a thirst and hunger for fortune, fame and recognition and will do downright anything to get what she wants. She will often go to the deepest extreme if necessary. She is a woman who is solely concerned with herself. Every step taken and every decision made is for the sole benefit of her upward mobility.

With a groupie, it's never about anyone else. It's about her. She's just taking an opportunity to fulfill her moment. Musical artists are just a character in the story and tomorrow it's gonna be Kanye West and then it'll be Lil' Wayne. It's a hustle, much like the rap game. She will often move from one artist to the next in order to obtain a lifestyle that she desires by performing sexual favors. She will continue to flaunt her assets in simple-minded "shake it up" videos. Within the world of Hip Hop, groupies are often referred to as b-tches, hoes, tricks, skeezas, golddiggers, hoochies and a variety of other demeaning names.

Ironically, rappers and directors aren't the only ones looking for action on the set. Often girl groupies, dazzled by celebrity, try to sleep their way to success. The stardom, fame, glitz and glamour are too hard for them to deny. So when an artist turns on the charm, it's hard to say no because for the girls it's a once in a lifetime chance. A lot of video girls are in hot pursuit to become the artist's number one honey. They get caught up in the hype of wanting to be the homeyloverfriend of a Nelly, T.I., or Webbie.

There are women who have no desire to grace the screen as a video girl, but choose to place an unrelenting focus on seducing the artist. These are women who will somehow make it past the masses, velvet ropes, the sturdy bouncer who guards the artist, through tight security and checkpoints into the most coveted inner sanctum. How? It's simple. The most glamorous groupies have virtually a free pass into every hot spot. One person said it best, "If you look like Halle Berry, dress like Mariah Carey, and have a body like Pam Grier, you will be let through every door."

Each week dozens of groupies make this similar journey to area nightclubs, hotels, parties, studios and hotspots all across town in hopes of preying upon artists. Many of these women pursue celebrities just so they can tell their girlfriends who they slept with. But for others, being with a celebrity provides entree into a world to which they wouldn't otherwise have access. The level of access is based upon the role the groupie decides to play.

If you thought groupies could easily be categorized, you couldn't be any further from the truth. There are a number of different kinds of groupies. You have the "lot lizards" (groupies who hang out where artists park their cars); "marry-mes" (groupies who want to be wives); "organization groupies" (those who work as staff in offices where artists frequent); "wives groupies" (those who try to get to artists through their wives); and the "high priced groupies" (those who amass a fortune at the expense of the artists).

While most groupies experience meager success, there are those high priced groupies who live the fabulous life. They shop on Rodeo Drive and Fifth Avenue, wear tight fitting Versace dresses, drive a convertible Mercedes CLK and sport Prada, Dolce & Gabanna and Jimmy Choo. They get a pass into every VIP lounge. They get escorted in limousines and arrive on airstrips after flying around on private jets in and out of major cities. They consume Dom Perignon, live in penthouse apartments and get manicures, pedicures and facials on a regular basis. They attend parties in the Hamptons and Hollywood Hills. They are able to afford this lavish lifestyle because they barter their bodies for cash. They are given $7000 for an evening with an athlete, $14,000 from a comedian, and another $5,000 from an artist on any given evening.

There are also less demanding women who are kept around solely as a crew's sexual jump off (sexual plaything). They are bounced around at anytime to fulfill the sexual desires of an artist and his entourage. They get cash for the sex and everyone is happy. For some, finding a sugar daddy is the ultimate goal. These women try to hit the jackpot and in their quest for the unattainable, will stop at nothing. One girl, desperate to find her fantasy man, had sex with a rapper, kept the condom after it was over and took a turkey baster to suck the semen out of it in order to insert it into her vagina for the purpose of getting pregnant.

These women will do anything they have to do in order to get what they want until the cash flow stops. Some groupies have taken advantage of a market that allows them to translate their sexual histories into lucrative tell-all book deals. Lately, the only thing you have to do to get a best-seller is have a few sexual escapades with a well-known rapper and take plenty of notes.

The most recognizable video hottie-turned-groupie is Karrine Steffans. Steffans, a former staple in various rap videos, authored *"Confessions of a Video Vixen,"* a memoir that details her relationships with some serious high rollers in the industry (DMX, Jay-Z, P.Diddy, Irv Gotti, Bobby Brown, Shaquille O'Neal and Ja Rule). She confesses that the sex was fueled by a stream of drugs and alcohol. Her sexual abilities were so well known, she was given the name Superhead.

Carmen Bryan, the mother of Nas' 10-year-old daughter Destiny, emerged with her autobiography *"It's No Secret: From Nas to Jay-Z, from Seduction to Scandal"* highlighting her sexual and personal encounters in the entertainment industry. The book details her experiences with celebrities such as Jay-Z, Allen Iverson and Wendy Williams among others. In addition, she claimed to have been intimate with the recently wedded Nas after he began his relationship with wife, singer Kelis.

Whether through a best-selling book or sexual behavior, groupies continue to pursue social status and the accumulation of material possession at the expense of their dignity and reputation.

Hip Hop Wives

It is common for rappers to lead double lives. In the world of Hip Hop the party never seems to stop. Countless rappers have become rich rhyming about what listeners may suppose are their lives. On stage, it's all about sex, money, power and an endless supply of women. But when the lights come up, many rappers go home to their wives which represent the final category which women squeeze into.

Wives and girlfriends fill another niche in rapper's lives. They are the ones who endure the most from their husbands and often suffer on multiple levels. In some respects, a wife is a more challenging role than being a groupie, stripper, or video ho. Not only do they have to endure the typical abuse and degradation heaped upon all Black women by rappers, but they must also put up with the cheating that is rampant in the Hip Hop industry.

It's a candy shop in these clubs and video sets. There are women gyrating in tiny outfits, drinking champagne and many rappers are torn between that life and their families. Just think about it. If you look at any current Hip Hop video, you'll find the setting adorned with glamorous, half-dressed (or less) women. So, in keeping up with that image, an artist having a woman on his arm that is as dazzling and beautiful as those that are on the set becomes a mandatory necessity. But for the woman who wants to remain true to her man, this can be challenging, especially, if she's not as young or as good looking as her video competition.

Often, treated as badly as or worse than the women their husbands rap about, the dream of becoming a superstar's better half dissolves into a nightmare of physical competition, humiliation and disenchantment. Despite this reality, very few wives divorce their rapper husbands. The thought of leaving the comforts that come along with the lifestyle is too much for some to handle.

The wives of Hip Hop celebrities have all the trappings of their husband's successes: huge diamond rings, impressive homes, and luxury cars. Many have even been fortunate to receive a first-rate business education from their spouses. As a result, countless wives and girlfriends have formed their own businesses (clothing lines, jewelry, cosmetics, modeling, reality TV, artist management companies, party planning, etc.). But there are some things these women want that just aren't for sale, and their real lives rarely match the fantasies of the girls who dream about marrying a successful rapper.

Why We Hate Black Women

Often alone while their husbands work far from home, these women raise children and manage households. Fighting insecurity, they try to keep the fires burning in the bedroom, though it's well-known that rappers play on the side. So, they often go along with the flow and accept what is considered "the norm" in the business.

Marriage doesn't even seem to maintain the same sanctity in the Hip Hop game when you have Eminem rapping about cutting his wife's throat and locking her in the trunk of a car. DMX is adamantly proud of his wife, in an interview, for being a trooper and enduring his infidelity, which is exemplified in his video *"What Them B-tches Want From Me?"* Ice-T, also married, still professes to be a real life pimp, exploiting the sexuality of other women. L.L. Cool J almost destroyed his marriage due to drugs and infidelity. However, he still features a different woman in his passionate surrealistic videos while assuring his wife and kids that it's all entertainment. Even Snoop Dogg allows his wife and three kids to rap along with his music as he refers to women as b-tches and hoes.

Beyond the private quarters of an artist's bedroom, Hip Hop wives seem to always catch a raw deal from media with all of its rumors, pretentious expectations and false allegations. As the late Biggie Smalls soon learned, some rappers consider the family fair game. In 1994, just four months after Biggie Smalls (Christopher Wallace) married Faith Evans, the king of all beefs erupted between Biggie and Tupac Shakur with Faith caught right in the middle.

After being shot several times in New York, Biggie's hometown, Tupac sought verbal revenge with his song *'Hit 'Em Up'*. The attack was aimed at both Biggie and his wife Faith. In the song, Tupac falsely accused Faith of sleeping with him while in California and escalated what became an 18 month feud that ultimately affected two coasts: the east coast and west coast. Rather than the Notorious B.I.G. retaliating, he instead created a video depicting the destructive end to his short-lived marriage with Faith due to her alleged infidelity. Apparently, Biggie's rep was more important to maintain than his marriage. Unfortunately, both were ultimately gunned down due to a turbulent atmosphere fostered by both artists. Meanwhile, Faith was left a widow and single parent to their child.

While there are countless horror stories of artists and their Hip Hop wives, there are also numerous great relationships as well. Even though it is certainly not a death sentence for women who decide to marry rappers, it has proven to come with its fair share of highs and lows.

Conclusion

Young black men are saturated by socially acceptable music that references black women in the most degrading ways possible. It should be expected that a fifteen year old boy that hears a rapper say "smack that b-tch" may consider doing it the next time he finds himself at odds with his girlfriend.

The musical influence extends well beyond the entertainment artists provide. Their messages are absorbed and mirrored in those who admire them. When the young Black male population constantly hears that it's not only ok, but right to treat women like sex objects, hoes, prostitutes and sub-humans, they take that to heart, and incorporate it into their own philosophy of life.

Continually hearing that it's totally acceptable to slap, beat and/or rape women, young men take on this persona as a value standard. Likewise, women who see themselves through the lens of others will willingly fall in line with the imagery and messages expressed in the music. But this has got to stop. It's time to call a spade a spade and deal with this issue, as a community, head on. Then, and only then, can real change occur.

Chapter 6

Black, Female and Mad As Hell

Hell knows no fury like a Black woman scorned.
~*Anonymous*

*S*everal years ago, while on my annual college speaking tour, I got hired to speak at Louisiana State University for their Black Love Week. It was one of the most anticipated events of the year. The school brought me in to talk about my book *Black Thighs, Black Guys & Bedroom Lies*. The title of the presentation created an enormous stir on campus. Twenty minutes before the event began the room was filled to capacity. By the time I started to speak it was standing room only.

The room was packed, the energy was high and I had everyone eating out of the palm of my hand. At the end of my 2-hour presentation I got a standing ovation. A few minutes after the students settled down, I opened up the floor for questions and answers. Several hands went up as I attempted to help solve personal relationship problems.

After about thirty minutes of good discussion, a very petite hand rose from the back of the room. The moment I acknowledged her, the small-framed college girl rose from her seat and began to share her disgust for many of the men on campus. She commented on how "All men are dogs", "They just can't be trusted" and "Black men ain't no good." Her comments immediately electrified the room.

During her three-minute critique, I stopped her midstream and told her that I wanted to immediately address her concerns. When I asked her for her name I was deeply concerned with her response. The young lady told me her name was 'Venom'. She had been given the nick-name by the men on campus because they said her attitude was as venomous as a snake.

Instantly, both rage and sorrow rose up within me upon hearing her response. Even though I was only a few years her elder, I felt fatherhood rise up within me. Like a disciplining parent, I said, "Don't you ever allow other people to call you out of your name. Don't you know that venom means poisonous, spiteful, malicious, resentful, bitter, antagonistic and deadly? Is that what you want to be known for?"

As I stood there all I could think about was the horrific social life of this young lady. But, as weeks passed I began to reflect on Black women as a group. Black women are the only women on the planet who are known for their attitudes.

White women are known for being pushovers and easy to deal with (sexually and relationally). Asian women are known for being very submissive. Latino women are known for being sexy and sensual. Unfortunately, Black women are known for being attitudinal and very hard to deal with. Granted, all of these are stereotypes and sweeping generalizations; however, they are all informed by some form of truth.

Now, I'm sure you can run down a long list of many sweet, happy-go-lucky and easy to get along with Black women. They are out there. In fact, they are everywhere. They are our mothers, daughters, sisters, girlfriends, wives, and friends. They have been wonderful examples of Black womanhood and should be praised for who they are.

With that said, we cannot ignore the salty, bitter, mean-spirited, attitudinal, angry, I can't wait to give him a piece of my mind Black woman who is glorified in the media. Hollywood has run the 'Angry Black Woman' caricature into the ground. *The Black woman with the bad attitude* has become the new signature breakout role. She typically gets the most airtime and most of the show centers around her foibles. Usually these are the ones you don't want to mess with because they will attempt to seek, kill and destroy.

While this infamous nasty attitude fails to work in a relationship, it is coveted in Hollywood. Telling people off at the slightest moment and being ready to fight over the most trivial issues is the rule of the day. Just consider Omarosa of the *Apprentice* and New York of *Flavor of Love*. These two women have become famous for their less desirable ways and they've benefited from a media frenzy consisting of television, talk radio and magazine covers.

The media's willingness to tell the story of the Black Woman's bitter reality is not an accident. The Angry Black Woman stigma has been a cornerstone of Hollywood's success for decades. It's not a new phenomenon. It's simply a new name put on an old socially constructed stereotype.

SAPPHIRE (Angry Black Woman)

The Sapphire caricature has always been a very hurtful stigma on Black women because it's been so difficult to escape. The slightest wince of emotion can trigger a barrage of unjustified attacks by those who view Black women as angry. While all of these stereotypes are harmful to society's view of Black women, the Sapphire (Angry Black Woman) stigma can arguably be considered the most damaging to Black women's careers, existing and future relationships, as well as their overall happiness.

The Sapphire caricature portrays Black women as evil, rude, loud, malicious, mean-spirited, abusive, stubborn, overbearing and hateful. She is frequently depicted as a tart-tongued, neck-twisting, finger-wagging, eye-rolling, eyebrow-raising, loud-mouthed, drama-filled, defiant sistah who specializes in emasculating men and putting in check anybody who dares step to her. She's a perpetual complainer. She seeks to take control and dominate everything. She has a high sensitivity for injustice no matter how big or small the incident. Ultimately, she's seen as miserable and looks to inflict her attitude of ingratitude on others.

Actress Ernestine Ward popularized the Sapphire image in the 1951 *Amos and Andy* television series. Ward played a character known as Sapphire who exhibited a very demeaning and spiteful personality toward her husband Kingfish. Kingfish was depicted as a lazy con artist who avoided work and took financial advantage of the ignorance of others. Their adversarial relationship and her ongoing verbal put-downs laid the foundation for her reputation.

What's unique about the Sapphire role is that this woman's very existence is predicated upon her ability to emasculate a Black man. Beyond her one-dimensional demeaning nature, the origins of this stereotype can be traced back to the Jezebel caricature. So, the Sapphire role is a hybrid depiction that uses both her anger and sex appeal to ultimately get what she wants.

While all other stereotypes began on the plantation, the Sapphire image can be traced back to World War II when many men were sent off to war and women were obligated to lead the home, work and handle all of the financial affairs. While this represented a burden of responsibility that women were not familiar with, many began to enjoy the independence that came along with it. In essence, it represented a shifting of power from the man to the woman which ultimately changed the way women viewed themselves in society.

Once men returned from the war, they were forced to deal with two harsh realities: 1) little to no work which affected their ability to provide, and 2) a new found independent female spirit. Both of these were viewed as challenges which had a great impact on the Black male psyche which, in turn, made him feel inferior and emasculated.

With racism, joblessness and poor skill sets as contributing factors, Black women became the primary protectors, providers and nurturers of the family within the home. As Black men's role in society began to diminish, Black women became dominant figures within the home and society which became a threat to male patriarchy. This ultimately fueled the riff between Black men and women; thus, the Sapphire was born.

Unfortunately, from the 1970s until as recently as today, the Sapphire Angry Black Woman has been the most dominant image of Black women in society. Like all of the other aforementioned stereotypes, Hollywood has built its empire on the backs of Black women. From Blaxploitation films to modern day Reality Shows, Black women have played the Sapphire character.

Black television's situational comedies were designed to get people to laugh as the angry Black woman, the Sapphire, insults and mocks Black men. Just consider the following examples:

Sanford and Son

Aunt Esther (also called Aunt Anderson) was a Sapphire character who was the Bible-swinging, angry nemesis and sister-in-law of the main character, Fred. They had a love-mostly hate relationship. Their adversarial verbal exchange was central to their interaction on the show. Fred would call Aunt Esther ugly and she would call him a "fish-eyed fool," "an old sucka," or a "beady-eyed heathen." They would often threaten to hit each other without ever fulfilling their promises. Not only did Aunt Esther demean Fred, she dominated her husband Woodrow, a mild-mannered alcoholic as well.

GoodTimes

This show featured the life of the Evans family in a Chicago housing project. The male-female tension was paramount in several characters. In many sitcoms, when there is a coon character, there is a Sapphire character to mock him. James Evans Jr., otherwise known as J.J., played the buffoon/coon who was constantly mocked by his sister Thelma. Another example of a Sapphire, was the neighbor, Willona Woods. While J.J. remained off limits, she belittled Nathan Bookman, the overweight superintendent, who she affectionately renamed 'Bugga'. She also put down a series of worthless boyfriends, an ex-husband, politicians, and other men with questionable morals and work ethics.

The Jeffersons

The Jeffersons featured an upper-middle class family that left the ghetto to live a better life. With their new privileged lifestyle came an antagonistic, back-talking, wisecracking Sapphire housekeeper by the name of Florence Johnston. Her relationship with George was very antagonistic and she would often tease him about his short stature, balding head and poor decisions.

Living Single

Living Single centered on six Black twenty-somethings consisting of four women and two men living in a brownstone in the heart of Brooklyn, New York. Even though the show would be described as a good portrayal of African Americans, it also had a negative stereotypical spin. The adversarial love/hate relationship between Maxine "Max" Shaw and Kyle Barker was very apparent. Their constant verbal sparring and demeaning disposition towards each other was blended with a strong sexual attraction. They maintained an on-again/off-again relationship that began at the end of the first season and continued until the end of the series.

Martin

Martin Lawrence's self-named sitcom '*Martin*' featured the infamous character Pamela (Pam) James who was known for her badmouthed, wisecracking relationship with radio disk jockey Martin. With six years of demeaning and belittling under her belt, she became typecast. So, it was easy for her to transition into the dominating, aggressive matriarch in the comedy, *Everybody Hates Chris*. What can Tichina Arnold say; she plays a good Angry Black Woman.

Beyond television sitcoms, there appeared to be no shortage of Angry Black Women depicted on television. Popular daytime 'trash talk' shows like *The Jerry Springer Show, The Jenny Jones Show, The Maury Povich Show,* and *The Ricki Lake Show* kept their ratings up for years by putting bitter Black women and the men who hate them on display.

The Sapphire image was further cemented in the minds of people because it was no longer considered fictitious entertainment. Rather, it is viewed as R-E-A-L-I-T-Y TV complete with a long list of Sapphire-like women. It seems like reality TV loves casting mean, sassy and strong Black women.

TV star Alicia Calloway was known for her temperament and finger wagging during an argument in 2001's *Survivor: The Australian Outback.* Coral Smith ruled with an iron tongue on MTV's *Real World/Road Rules Challenge: The Inferno.* She browbeat one female cast mate so badly that she challenged Smith to a fight. Then there's Omarosa Manigault-Stallworth of *The Apprentice,* who rode the angry-black-woman stereotype into a small bankroll and an extended moment of fame.

Omarosa, was portrayed (and intentionally acted) as a cross between a Jezebel, a hypersexual flirt and seductress, and a bitter, aggressive Sapphire. Both Black and White audiences interpreted Omarosa as conniving, lazy, selfish, fake, overly-ambitious, uppity, ungrateful and paranoid. As notoriously deplorable as Omarosa's image and behavior was, it could not compete with VH1's reality show sensation Tiffany Pollard A.K.A. New York.

The '*I Love New York I and II*' reality show was VH1's highest-rated reality show to date. *From Flavor of Love I and II* to both of her own shows, New York captured the attention of both Black and White audiences. From young Black girls in the inner cities of America to middle-aged White corporate female executives, all remained glued to their television sets weekly as Tiffany cursed, fought, sexed, emasculated, and totally demeaned herself into a whirlwind of super stardom. The Jezebel-Sapphire Hybrid role that she mastered on screen depicted the raunchiest, most hyper-sexual, attitudinal, mean-spirited, masculine, and violently aggressive behavior exhibited by any reality show personality in the history of television.

Why We Hate Black Women

As if one angry Black woman wasn't enough, VH1 found it necessary for Tiffany to share the screen with her number one partner in crime, the infamous 'Sister Patterson.' As bad as Tiffany's lioness behavior was, she purred like a kitten in the presence of her malicious, cold and calculating, Darth Vader-like church-going mother. Striking fear in the heart of everyone who entered her presence, Sister Patterson basked in the glory of her deplorable display.

Television has done a poor job of offering adequate depictions of Black women beyond the one-dimensional roles of the mammy, Jezebel, the tragic mulatto or Sapphire. So, if you ever decide to consider the big screen for a little bit of relief, think again. Angry Black Women have proven to render Hollywood corporate executives a substantial profit.

From rapper Eve's shouting and tongue-lashing role as Terri in *The Barbershop I and II* to Gabrielle Unions role as Eva in *Deliver Us From Eva*", to Lynn Whitfield's role as Brandy in a *A Thin Line Between Love and Hate*, the role of angry Black women appear to have no apparent end in sight.

These images are so ingrained in society and so damaging to Black women that the "angry Black woman" tag gets slapped on any African-American woman in a position of power who stands for something. Even First Lady Michelle Obama is considered a bitter, selfish, uppity, ungrateful, overly-ambitious Sapphire. She has even been nicknamed "Omarosa Obama." This demonstrates how the Sapphire caricature has *transcended* its association with emasculating haters of Black men to fall upon any woman who takes a stand or position on anything.

Unfortunately, the Sapphire caricature has negatively affected Black women's role in society, their upward mobility in the corporate world, the quality of their relationships and the way they are perceived by others. This particular defamation of character is by far the most damaging of all existing stereotypes today.

Nobody Likes An Angry Black Woman

Since Black women and their attitudes are at the center of many heated discussions nationwide, I thought it would be fitting to delve further into the topic to get to the bottom of the issue. I wanted to find out how Black women are perceived based upon people's personal experiences because beyond the media hype, this type of woman does exist. Once again, they are out there. In fact, they are everywhere. Some of them are our mothers, daughters, sisters, girlfriends, wives and friends.

My journey was quite an adventurous one. From phone interviews, to group discussions, blog posts, book research, and campus visitations, I've collected a multitude of responses from Black men, White men, and women alike. The following responses stood out the most:

We ARE seen as angry, nasty, hostile and rude and for the most part it's true. I, as a black woman, have encountered these types of "nasty" women educated or uneducated and it really bothers me. We complain about how we can't find good men and how men are intimidated by this, that and the third, but in reality the blame can fall on us too...we're so concerned with other women of other races that we don't even try to focus on us. We are too consumed by anger at all these other races of women stealing "our" men that it just makes us these "angry" black women.

If we just quit worrying about others and focused on growing mentally, spiritually, emotionally, physically, financially etc. we'd have better relationships. We get a bad rap, because we allow it. You can't want to be respected when you disrespect others as well as yourself. I try my very best to not be that "angry" black woman. I understand that it's a tough world out there, but at the same time I know how to stand my ground and be that strong black woman, without belittling others and being rude and nasty.

Nadine, Nurse, TX (Black Female)

What Black women call strong, men call nasty...and it has spilled over into our attitudes and dispositions. When I was a waitress in college, I

Why We Hate Black Women

used to HATE waiting on Black women. Invariably, they were hostile, rude, picky, never satisfied and didn't tip well. They were the worst customers.

Susanne, Engineer, NJ (Black Female)

...And that's why 'We Hate Black Women'...cause they're rude, ignorant and nasty. There are different classes of nasty...It's not all the same.....They're either Ghetto Nasty (rude and ignorant), Educated Nasty (arrogant and haughty), Sanctified Nasty (self-righteous and judgmental), Baby Mama Nasty (bitter and jealous) or Fat and Nasty (low self-esteem, lazy and blames men for preferring smaller women).

Tasha, Account Rep, VA (Black Female)

A black woman's attitude is a TURN OFF. There is a time and place to express your feelings and emotions, but to get loud and ignorant just to be over the top...isn't appealing. Wagging the finger and doing the head bop. While saying..."MMMMMMHMMMMM ". I am the man in the relationship so I refuse to date/marry someone who thinks they control me and my character while attempting to belittle me just to get a point across. I'll pass...and I have passed..and I will continue to pass. Let somebody else have that woman.

James, Attorney, MD (Black Male)

Sistas, you have competition, you betta, change your act, women from other ethnic backgrounds are coming strong, they have everything you have without the Attitude-

John, College Student, AZ (Black Male)

I am a white man who is getting divorced from a black woman. She has the WORST attitude of any woman I have ever met. She managed to do a pretty good job of hiding it before we were married, but she turned it loose after we said our "I do's". She is constantly angry and nothing I or anyone else says or does will help. I tried and hung in there for 7 years and she told me she didn't love and wanted to leave me 3x for no apparent reason - I was very good to her and loved her with all my heart. I even offered to go to counseling with our pastor but she refused. The first 2 times I hung in there because I am a Christian and I believe that when you give your word in the marriage vows, you should stick to it. But I have never seen such a horrible attitude or anger problem in a person in my entire life.

I regret ever meeting her. Even though she is very physically beautiful, the attitude just kills it. I went to see my pastor after she announced she wanted to leave me, and after talking to him, he even said to just let her go and later on find someone else. We are not called by God to be someone's doormat. Her nasty attitude has made her enemies and cost her jobs before. She was once fired from a very good paying job because of her bad attitude. This didn't change her, however, she just learned to "play nice" a little better when the help is around.

I have also talked to a number of other white guys who have dated black girls and they have all said the same thing - that the black women they dated have terrible attitudes and anger management problems. Most of these white guys say they would never do it again. This is very bad news for the black chicks out there who have developed a liking for white men. We are getting wise to your attitude! This is why many white men won't date black women. It used to be the race issue. Now that's pretty much dead. It's pretty much ok in white society to date outside your race now pretty much everywhere except in the extreme rural south. So if white guys are saying no or not interested in you now, its probably because they are wise to the attitude thing. I hear the locker room talk. And that's what we are saying. We talk to the brothas too. And they are saying it as well.

So ladies, you better tone it down if you want to have a chance with self respecting white guys. Word is getting out amongst white men about your attitudes and many of us are now wary and cautious about dating you because of others' experiences with this problem.

Why We Hate Black Women

I really don't get it. You black ladies are extremely beautiful (well at least some of you are) but the attitude thing just totally kills it. After my divorce is final I will consider dating another black woman but at the FIRST sign of attitude, I am outta there so fast she won't know what happened. Life is too short to be some angry black chick's doormat. And 99% of the time, she was mad at something or someone else but taking it out on me.

I am an educated (master's degree) very attractive and very well built white guy (former bodybuilder) who can do much better. Like I said before, I would consider dating black women again but I will not tolerate attitude one bit in the future.

If everyone, black and white alike, would just treat others as you want to be treated, this wouldn't even be an issue.

Anonymous (White Male)

By now, some of you are pissed off and offended at what you just read. You are probably thinking up a long laundry list of reasons why these people are sell-outs, out of touch with their Blackness, unworthy to be taken serious, or totally disqualified from even having an opinion at all. Some of you are probably mentally defending why Black women are the way they are and why Black men should understand it and just deal with it.

Meanwhile, there are those of you who are in total agreement with these statements. You see elements of truth in everything that has been said. In fact, you may have personally exhibited some of these behaviors yourself or know someone who has. In either case, you acknowledge the existence of the Angry Black Woman.

I think it's safe to say that there are angry, bitter, miserable and attitudinal Black women in the world. Honestly, I don't see how anyone could deny their existence. The bigger issue to discuss is why there are so many angry Black women. Let's take a closer look.

Why Are There So Many Angry Black Women?

Before I attempt to answer the question, I think it's important that we have a thorough understanding of the word Angry. For decades the word has been used so loosely that it has placed Black women in a box that has unfairly described their attitudes and behavior. In *Roget's Super Thesaurus* Angry has a lengthy list of synonyms; however, there are a few that stand out. A short list of words and phrases mentioned includes mad, annoyed, bitter, displeased, provoked, venomous and explosive.

Immediately, this list reveals two things. First, each word is different in its meaning. For instance, annoyed is drastically different from bitter. Explosive is certainly different from displeased. So, each word that is outwardly expressed comes with a unique set of feelings and emotions.

Second, each word represents a different level of expression. An explosive woman may erupt at a moment's notice. Whereas, a displeased woman may exhibit a milder response that reaches a boiling point over a period of time. In essence, no two women who are given the label Angry Black Woman are the same. So, it is unfair to pigeonhole all Black women and lump them into a category that doesn't fitly describe who they are.

Now that we have a better understanding of the word 'Angry', let's look at some possible causes of Black women's anger. Regardless of what you may have been told, Black women did not come out of the womb angry. There are a myriad of reasons that contribute to the anger we see in Black women; however, there are four contributors to seriously consider.

1. Stolen Childhood

According to social researcher Kay Hymowitz, over 70 percent of Black children live in single-parent households. Single-parenting, particularly in urban areas where financial hardship is a reality, typically presents a number of challenges.

According to the Centers for Disease Control, poverty within urban settings puts children at an increased risk of physical violence including school fights, gangs, injury from weapons, violent crimes, and drug activity. Economically, many have been forced to grow up too soon: caring for siblings while adults are at work, running errands, working a job while in school and handing over earnings to contribute to household expenses. One distraught girl who lived this lifestyle said "I never had a chance to play with Barbie dolls..."

In relationships, many have been exposed to dating violence in addition to forced sex (rape and molestation) at a young age, which in turn has robbed them of their innocence. One Black girl interviewed said "I got raped and was molested over a period of seven years and became suicidal. And I'm only fifteen." Others have engaged in premature sex at a young age and face an increased risk of HIV infection. How? Many have dated promiscuous males, and older males with longer sexual histories, who may have exposed them to infection. Others have fallen victim to the down low phenomenon (men who have sex with both men and women but categorize themselves as heterosexual).

Lastly, there are women who suffer from self-esteem issues inflicted upon them by peers due to unnecessary ridicule. Disparaging remarks about their hair, complexion, body shape, weight, physical features, fashion, hygiene, and countless other things profoundly contribute to their poor sense of self. All these factors contribute to the anger, attitude or aggressive disposition young Black girls have while growing up.

2. Negative Relationships With The Men In Their Lives

It is no surprise that quite a few Black women are disgusted with their relationships. While many can attest to wonderful relationships with their significant others, countless Black women are frustrated, tired and angry about the treatment they've received from men. From their fathers to their lovers, pain has been a constant theme in their relationships. Consider the following explanation for "bitterness," which was shared with me by an interviewee:

"Well, personally, I know I adopted my "nasty" attitude as a defense mechanism in response to my no-good, unloving, cheatin', lying, good-for-nothing father (who just happens to be Black-- which proves that you Black men, like everyone else, have problems, too) who always, treated me, my mother and my sister terribly. Because of how he treated me, I learned to speak up for myself. I say what I mean instead of being fake or letting anyone walk all over me. If that makes me a b-tch or considered to have an "attitude," then I'll be that. Inevitably, given the same circumstances, I believe I would have been this way regardless of the color of my skin. "

Sadly, there a millions of responses just like this from women who struggle with suffering that originated in their bad relationship or their lack of relationship with their father. Many suffer from what Jonetta Rose Barras, author of *Whatever Happened To Daddy's Little Girl?* calls 'Fatherless Woman Syndrome'. The lack of a father in a woman's life may contribute to her unexplained anger and her rage which she may express through addictions to drugs, alcohol, food, sex and other objects. The illness of depression, which is a natural outgrowth of anger, can also set in which leads to all sorts of personal problems and disasters.

Let's think about this for a moment. If women receive such poor treatment from their own flesh and blood, how much worse could it be with a love interest? Let's take a look. Black women have been lied to, cheated on, humiliated, disrespected, abused, beaten, betrayed, rejected, taken for granted and abandoned all in the name of love. From one relationship to the next, they have endured less than desirable treatment.

While some experience total neglect, others are verbally, emotionally and physically abused. Meanwhile, women have become frustrated because they've been forced to become do-it-yourself women while their men sit around and do nothing all day or struggle with their job to make ends meet.

With one bad relationship after another, there's no wonder why Black women are so mad. Women are pissed off and walk around with a big chip on their shoulder and justifiably so. Men in their lives have hurt them, sliced open bloody wounds and have poured salt in them. These are men who are partially responsible for the hard and emotionally callous women they complain about. The sad part is that Black women will continue to be angry and bitter as long as they continue to deal with men who exhibit such behavior.

3. Legacy of Abandonment

There is a nation of single Black women in America today. These women do not fit a typical description. They represent a large cross section of women. They range in age, education, occupation, financial obtainment and social status. No matter how diverse their experiences may be, there's one chord that binds them all together. It is the stigma of what it means to be Black and female in America.

The term 'single' has almost become synonymous with Black women, so much so, that sistahs are beginning to plot out their lives in ways that do not include a man. They want to obtain the job, the house, the car, the ability to travel and even the child without the presence of a man. It's not that they don't want a man. Rather, they've gotten used to being alone and have moved on with their lives.

There are families of women, from great-grandmothers on down, who have remained un-partnered for generations. Are they content with this situation? No, they're pissed. They have been forsaken by their own men. But beyond being un-partnered, Black women are upset about the affects of being un-partnered.

First, Black women are forced to fend for themselves. They're tired of raising kids, cooking meals, doing homework, mowing the lawn and paying bills with no assistance from the very men who helped put them in these situations. The emotional, physical, and financial hardship that men have placed on women is almost indescribable.

Second, this abandonment has profoundly shaped how women participate in relationships. While in some instances women react to abandonment issues by "loving harder" in obsessive and unhealthy ways, in other cases, women build thick walls around their hearts and minds that prevent any well intentioned man from entering in. They shut down all emotions and intimacy because they have been made vulnerable to men's ill treatment and behavior for years.

These failed relationships have taught women to either prepare to be alone or prepare to be hurt. This dubious expectation in men has caused them to embrace the all too familiar cultural clichés that we constantly hear: 'I can do bad all by myself,' 'I don't need no man' and 'I'm a strong Black independent woman.' Though these phrases sound empowering, they are often defense mechanisms to hide their internalized hurt and pain.

4. Attacked On All Fronts

Black women are sick and tired of being disrespected and attacked by the world. Just think about it. Their fathers leave them, their uncles molest them, their lovers cheat on and abuse them, comedic actors ridicule them, and media journalists negatively label them.

Who could forget the infamous comments made by shock jock Don Imus when he referred to the Rutgers University women's basketball team, which is comprised of eight African-American and two White players, as "nappy-headed hoes" immediately after the show's executive producer, Bernard McGuirk, called the team "hard-core hoes." Later, former *Imus* sports announcer Sid Rosenberg, who was filling in for sportscaster Chris Carlin, said: "The more I look at Rutgers, they look exactly like the [National Basketball Association's] Toronto Raptors."

Fox News Network's anchor Megyn Kelly referred to Michelle Obama as Barack Obama's 'baby mama'. The sexist and racially-insensitive term also ran on the bottom of the Fox News screen during the discussion. Anyone born in the 21st century knows the term 'baby mama' refers to an unmarried woman who has had a child. The statement is demeaning because of the obvious negative connotation. They are seen as desperate, gold digging, emotionally starved, shady women who had a baby because of irresponsibility or to keep a man.

By labeling Michelle Obama as a 'baby mama' is an attack on all Black women. Why? Michelle Obama is looked at as a symbol of Black womanhood. She represents the character, strength, intelligence, success and beauty of Black women. So, a culturally insensitive attack on her is a sweeping indictment against all Black women.

To add further insult to injury, all Black women are looked at as angry when viewed through the lens of White America. Fox News' syndicated columnist Cal Thomas was quoted as saying, "Look at the image of angry black women on television. Politically you have Maxine Waters of California, liberal Democrat. She's always angry every time she gets on television. Cynthia McKinney, another angry black woman. And who are the black women you see on the local news at night in cities all over the country. They're usually angry about something. They've had a son who has been shot in a drive-by shooting. They are angry at Bush. So you don't really have a profile of non-angry black women."

The major problem with the media's attack on Black women is that people's perceptions, prejudices, and opinions are often shaped by information they receive from television, radio and print media. As a result, their interaction with Black women is often flush with stereotypical undertones that do not go unnoticed. It seems that no matter what Black women do, they can't catch a break.

In addition to the prior four contributing factors mentioned, are myriad legitimate issues that must seriously be considered: racial injustice, financial hardships, missed educational opportunities, over-extended responsibilities and obligations, unfulfilled expectations, exposure to other angry Black women, and the overall difficulties of life. All of these issues compounded, one on top of the other, can influence a negative attitude in a person.

From Hurt To Healed

While doing research I came across a YouTube video clip of *Divorce Court*. I was immediately struck by the title of the video (probably edited by a Black male). It was entitled 'Wild, Loud Sapphire Black Woman Routinely Beats Her Simple Husband.'

As I watched the two-part video series, I witnessed a very volatile, explosive and physically abusive Black woman express why she was divorcing her husband. They had been married for 1.5 years and shared a child together. During their short marriage, he cheated on her multiple times with multiple women. He even got another woman pregnant while his own wife was pregnant carrying their first-born child.

During the court case, the wife began to describe the instances during which she would beat on her husband at home, in the grocery store, at the WIC office and other places throughout town. One time, when she caught him at another woman's house, she ran to her car, put on her running shoes and then chased him down the street with a baseball bat.

While the studio audience (witnesses in the courtroom) and viewers at home found the episode entertaining, it left me disturbed. My problem with the video is that most people who see it will view her as the problem. Her boisterous disposition on television will cause her to be perceived as a raging lunatic that no one could ever empathize with. As horrendous as her behavior was, the real culprit is the cheating husband; however, his trifling ways are overshadowed by the roar of his loud-mouthed wife. Unfortunately, the scenario is all too familiar.

Behind the anger, bitterness, rage and attitude exhibited in Black women is tremendous hurt and pain. So many sistahs are emotionally wounded and as the saying goes 'hurt people, hurt

115

people'. In other words, their attitude, hurtful words and actions are usually a result of their own internalized pain. They may erupt with inappropriate emotions because particular thoughts, words, actions or circumstances trigger past wounds. So, they react and those around them become the victims of harsh tones and fits of rage. In essence, because she suffers, everyone around her suffers as well.

The Angry Black Woman is like a can of soda that has been carelessly handled. You've seen it before. A can of soda that is not delicately handled may explode into a gushing fountain of fizz when opened. What makes this happen? Well, every time you open a soda can without shaking it, you hear a familiar popping sound. That is the sound of pressure inside the can being released because soft drinks are canned under pressure to help keep them carbonated.

When you shake a can, the carbon dioxide at the top of the can is spread throughout the liquid creating pressurized bubbles that rumble within the can. So, when the can is opened, instead of a pop of air escaping, a burst of liquid is released resulting in a sticky mess and remnant stains. Black women are under intense pressure as previously mentioned. When they are constantly mistreated and mishandled, they explode. Their sticky mess runs all over the one who mishandles them.

Among the complexities of being Strong Black Women is the need to appear strong at all times. The slightest sign of vulnerability (crying, pouting or whining) gives them the appearance of weakness. So, in an attempt to mask their weakness from the world, they internalize their hurts and pains and instead respond with a more aggressive approach which they believe is a sign of strength.

The problem with that approach is that it rubs people the wrong way. Not only do those who mishandle them get caught in the explosion but anyone in sight who they see as a potential threat may find themselves in a mess. So, the girl in line at the bank, the grocery store clerk, the waiter at the restaurant, the guy who notices them from across a crowded room or any innocent bystander can easily fall victim to the wrath of an Angry Black Woman.

In the end, the one who suffers the most is the Angry Black Woman. First, her romantic relationships suffer. She wants to be in a loving relationship but in order to get there she must let her guard down. Unfortunately, some just aren't willing to take that risk so they often end up alone or in another bad relationship.

Second, her personal reputation suffers. Once people get a taste of her unpleasant disposition she's marked for life. Word will quickly spread and the 'ABW' (Angry Black Woman) stigma will forever remain on her whether the process of change takes place or not. The reality is that people don't care why certain women have attitudes. They just don't want to be bothered. By the time they get around to caring, they're gone.

The failure of romantic, platonic and family relationships increases her isolation. Family members, friends, co-workers, associates and complete strangers begin to emotionally/physically distance themselves in an attempt to maintain their own peace. The only way for this cycle to end is for these women to go through a healing process.

Even though your childhood, your father, your past relationships and other factors contributed to your pain, you are responsible for your own healing. Your healing ultimately starts and ends with you. It won't be easy. It may take some time to heal. It may be hard to let go of things and forgive. It may be hard on your spirit, soul and body. But, in the end, you'll be a better person for it. So, no longer allow the seed of bitterness and anger to grow inside of you. Rather, plant the seed of love, joy and happiness so that the world can see your light, rather than misinterpret your pain for darkness.

Chapter 7

Black Women Who Hate On Other Women

Can't we all just get along?
~Rodney King

*I*t's New Year's Eve. The night is still young. Savannah looks into a mirror as she meticulously places the finishing touches of makeup on her face. She's ready to go. She arrives at a beautifully lit restaurant full of people celebrating the coming of a new year. People are sipping on drinks, dancing on the dance floor and sitting at tables conversing with one another.

Savannah walks through the door looking radiant with her hair pinned up wearing a black spaghetti-strapped dress that drapes the floor with every step. While visually scanning the room for her blind date she spots a table of three women and two men with an available chair. She casually approaches the table and asks, "Excuse me. Is anyone sitting here?" The two men react as if they have been practicing their response for several weeks. In unison, they both say "No... please... join us."

Savannah sits down. But, no sooner than her behind hits the chair, the three women stare her down as if she just hog spit in each of their faces. They angrily whispered to one another "she has the nerve to sit down here." Savannah quickly turns from joyful and carefree to emotionally callous. She looks the women in their eyes and speaks a nonverbal form of communication expressed through a look on her face that says" Heck yeah, I'm single and desperate and have no morals. And as soon as one of you turns your back, I'm gonna flirt my butt off and take your man." Savannah then gets up from the table as the women continue to roll their eyes. As she walks away, one woman says to the others "I can't stand women like her...please...hmm."

Can you guess what movie this scene is from? Okay, I'll tell you. It's Terry McMillan's 1995 *Waiting To Exhale*. What's interesting about this illustration is that the entire interaction lasts less than 10 seconds. But within that short span of time so much takes place. It is reminiscent of what happens with women each and every day.

A woman walks into a room full of other women and The Games Begin. Words don't need to be spoken. Gestures don't need to be made. Just the mere presence of a woman automatically poses a potential threat to everyone else in the room. Instantly, a line is drawn in the sand, the enemy is swiftly identified and the match begins. Conversely, men can be in the same room and be totally oblivious to what is going on. Meanwhile, women have already assessed the situation, devised a strategy and have even come up with contingency plans should anything go wrong, all while quietly sitting in the comfort of their seats.

Does this ring a bell? You walk into a room and feel the stare of piercing eyes penetrating the depths of your soul. You hear subtle sounds of other women sucking their teeth, breathing hard, and talking under their breath. You feel them staring at you like green-eyed monsters (jealousy), but every time you look their way their eyes simultaneously move in another direction. You know they're hating on you because of how you look, dress, or carry yourself. You feel like saying 'WHAT?! DO YOU HAVE A PROBLEM?" Instead, you keep your composure and say nothing. However, the incident further solidifies why you choose not to deal with too many women.

It's been said that when you have a group of ten or more women, of any ethnicity, in a setting, it is guaranteed that at least three of them do not like each other. Six have gossiped behind each other's back, four have had arguments, two may have been with the same man, five are close-knit and at least one is oblivious to the group's dynamics.

It is no secret that women are very careful of who they befriend. In fact, from my personal experience, the women I know have a very small select group of female friends. Many of them would rather deal with a man than another woman. Typically, misogyny is a term thrown around in reference to men who hate women; however, I don't think there is a term to specifically describe the fact that there are women who hate women as well. The obvious contention between women raises the age old question asked by Rodney King during the 1992 L.A. riots, "Can't we all just get along?"

Competing With The Enemy

Women have looked upon each other as competition for years. But this gender struggle is not exclusive to Black women. African-Americans haven't cornered the market on "hating," gossip and cat-fights among women. Women of all nationalities are known for occasionally treating each other with contempt. Regardless of culture, women often contend with issues that are specific to their gender. However, there are particular issues that are specific to the Black experience in America. It is my intention to cover both.

Physical attractiveness is a huge area of competition for women. Why? Beauty is one of the most coveted things that women strive for and men seek. So, it is no surprise that women often judge each other from the outside in rather than the inside out. These are women who have the ability to evaluate a woman from head-to-toe. They can size up another woman's physical assets in a matter of seconds.

Many factors are taken into consideration such as their hair, facial features, complexion, body type, weight, clothing and accessories. So, women judge their own self-worth based upon how they measure up to other women, rather than through their own personalized standard of beauty.

For instance, a woman may be fine with her size ten until her girlfriend confidently sports a size eight. All of a sudden, the woman feels a sudden need to drop 2 or more dress sizes in order to feel a sense of personal security. She also feels like she has to maintain an edge over her girlfriend no matter how slight it may be. In her mind, being more physically attractive increases her worth and chances of either finding or keeping companionship.

Women often observe each other's skin, hair, stomach, waistline, legs, breasts and buttocks. While some admire the beauty in others, some automatically hate on other women because the other woman possesses something that they may not have. According to Cassandra A. George Sturges, author of *The Illusion of Beauty: Why Women Hate Themselves & Envy Other Women*: "On a daily basis most women do not compete for professional achievement, academic success, or promotions the way they compete with each other for the attention of men. Somehow you feel that the man you love would be willing to give up every moment he ever shared with you ... just to taste her, to hold her and touch her because ... God must have awakened early in the morning to sculpt her and He pieced you together with her leftovers after six days without sleeping. She reminds you of everything that you want but could never have."

The fact of the matter is that some women are just considered more physically appealing than others. Unfortunately, women are often judged by physical characteristics they have little control over. The more attractive woman has no more control over her looks than the less attractive woman. However, conflict is perpetuated based upon this one dynamic. In many cases, the more attractive one is resented and made the victim of all forms of cattiness, snide remarks, eye rolls, cold shoulders and unwarranted hostility.

Janeen, a 39-year old telecommunications specialist said,

"Unfortunately, I have been hated on by other black females. In high school, bad girls wanted to fight me because 'I thought I was cute' when in reality they thought I was cute. In early adulthood I had females dislike me because they may have been involved with men who showed interest in me or they always had something to say about the way I carried myself."

I find it quite interesting that some women will have no problem with another woman until they perceive that other woman to have even a slight advantage over them. Once these women perceive that slight advantage in another, they feel threatened. Just think about it; women often use code words or loaded terms that hide how they really feel about other women they deem as competition. You've heard it all before.

For instance, every man that I know who's ever heard a woman refer to another woman as 'cute' or 'pretty' may certainly think that she is, but deep down inside they're saying 'I know I look better than her'. Comparatively, when some women say that another woman is 'alright' or 'ok', often she really does look good but they may choose not to admit it. Some women will pick other attractive women apart and reduce them down to their most finite features.

Typical comments that I've heard over the years are "Tyra Banks has a big forehead." "Halle Berry is plain looking." "Nia Long ain't all that. She's just like any other pretty Black chick that you'd see walking down the street." Meanwhile, men go cuckoo for cocoa puffs over these women.

Several years ago, I was having Sunday dinner at a friend's house where several couples were visiting. While we were all casually watching a movie on television Nia Long appeared in one of the scenes and two of the husbands began making grunting noises, inappropriate gestures and distasteful comments about how

beautiful and sexy she was. Meanwhile, the wives became furious and felt totally disrespected, and rightfully so.
One woman interviewed said,

"I don't like it when my boyfriend looks at other girls and comments on how attractive they are. Real life or TV or magazines—makes no difference. I admit it. It's a natural response among girls. Girls like being 'the other woman' thus, if we let our man go gaga over that other girl, that means we let that other girl win this so called underlying competition."

In addition to competing with their fellow women, whom they encounter each and every day, women may find themselves competing with the media images that society is constantly bombarded with. Many of these visuals have succeeded in lowering a woman's sense of value. They often feel like they've been replaced and thrown away. Whether it is a television sitcom character, a video vixen dancing in a video, a prostitute standing on a city corner, a stripper swinging from a pole, a nude model displayed in a magazine, or a porn actress performing in a sex flick, women are often devastated by their partner's decision to visually stray.

Each time a man looks at a live image or still frame picture of a naked or scantily clad woman, it's an insult to the woman he's with. To her, he's basically saying, this is what really turns me on, not the woman beside me. With a plentiful assortment of beautiful faces, thighs, breasts, hips, and behinds to choose from, many women feel as if they simply can't compete. A woman feels forced to measure up to women she doesn't even know just to fight for her man's attention.

Concerning female competition, men are often at the root. Either a woman is trying to gain the attention of a man, pursue a man, or keep the man she currently has. Concerning looks, a woman may not know how to beat her rival because the rival is in no more control over her appearance than she is.

However, women compete with each other in various ways. Their limitation in one area is often overcompensated for with strength in another area. When they can't compete with other women physically, they often create an alluring and irresistible niche that will intentionally separate them from the rest of other women in order to maintain a competitive edge.

Some women will attempt to get to a man's heart by perfecting their culinary skills and regularly cooking to a man's personal delight. Others will seek to cultivate sexual talents by reading sex magazines, watching porno movies and consulting other men. Many are known to obsessively diet and workout in an effort to sculpt a perfect body that can make any man drop to his knees. Several women have even resorted to letting a man live in her home rent-free, buying him expensive gifts, baby-sitting his children and continually lending him money amongst many other things.

Depending on the woman, some will even deceive a man into thinking that she's on birth control and intentionally get pregnant in order to trap a man into a relationship. What they don't understand is that if a man doesn't want to commit to you, he's certainly not likely to commit to your baby. The techniques that women use to snare a man are endless. Because many women are very conscious of how other women think and behave, they are very cautious of these women, especially in the presence of their man.

Stay Away From My Man

Many women do not believe that men are biologically capable of resisting another woman's sexual allure. In fact, if a man doesn't partake in the forbidden nectar of another woman who happens to be drop-dead gorgeous, it was the woman who most likely determined the outcome. Generally speaking, platonic relationships between men and women exist because the woman isn't interested in having sex with the man. So, many women believe that if another beautiful woman really wanted and pursued her man, he would be hers for the taking.

Just think. When a woman enters into a room and your man's eyes immediately gravitate towards her, the competitive line is drawn. You may pretend not to notice but inside you feel threatened by his behavior. The habitual act of looking at other women can often cause feelings of intimidation, insecurity, inadequacy, low self-esteem and competition.

All of a sudden, you feel replaceable because every time you look up your man's attention is elsewhere. His actions have forced you to compare yourself to every half-way decent looking woman who comes anywhere near your peripheral vision. Why? You are vulnerable to another woman stealing your man. That's right. Women can be just as ruthless and cut-throat as some men. Even though men are referred to as dogs for cheating on their significant others, more often than not they're having sex with other women.

On the flip side, you know as a woman, you potentially have the power of taking another woman's man if you really wanted to. If you have integrity, you will send him back home to his woman. If you don't, you will help destroy whatever is left of the sisterhood that binds you all together. Interestingly, while a part of you is disgusted by a man's doggish ways, a part of you is flattered that you made another woman's man look at you in a way that was only meant for her. In all reality, you may have made him want you.

How can you make another man want you? Well, some don't have to do anything. Some men are just drawn to you because of what you naturally exhibit. There is nothing intentionally done to allure him into your arms. On the other hand, some women are just plain trifling. They will go to extremes to win the glance of a man. The most obvious way is with their choice of provocative attire.

So many women get upset when men make derogatory comments about them and their body parts. They come out the house exposing their cleavage, stomach, legs, and thongs and have the nerve to get mad when someone makes a disparaging statement. Personally, I find it to be ridiculous. You knew your nipples were poppin' out of your shirt and your cleavage was exposed all the way down to your areola when you left the house. You knew that the combination of your low riding hip huggers and your g-string would reveal the crack of your behind to every eager onlooker. You wore what you wore on purpose.

Most women dress this way for one of three possible reasons. If she's single, it's done to get the attention of a man, whether he's spoken for or not. If she's married, it might be done to visually entice her own man. However, some do it to see if they've still got it. It can't be denied that women love attention. Thirdly, whether single or married, some women dress for other women. Yeah, that's right! It's an intimidation tactic. She will accentuate her greatest assets in front of other women to make it known that she's a threat and should not be messed with. And it often works. It causes some women to feel insecure about their bodies.

Women enjoy torturing each other with their beauty. It's a psychological game that's played. They know that the more physically appealing they are, the bigger the advantage they have over less desirable women. The winner of the game is determined by whoever receives the most attention and the ultimate prize is the acquisition of a man, whether he's taken or not.

The problem with this competition is that it often makes some women believe they are superior to other women if they are physically more attractive. But the superiority that they profess quickly subsides once they come to grips with a very harsh reality. While their beauty may ensure their ability to get a man, it never ensures their ability to keep a man. Some of the most beautiful women in the world could not keep their male partners from desiring or even having sexual affairs with other women. Just ask Halle Berry.

No matter how beautiful one may be, the possibility of infidelity is very real. Knowing this, many women keep their male partners on a short leash and all women at a distance. Unfortunately, far too many women have used the power of their femininity to steal another woman's man.

The reasons for their indiscretions vary significantly. Some get involved in relationships with committed men because they truly desire another woman's man and stop at nothing to get what they want. Others cheat because of a perceived shortage of qualified men in the dating pool. Since all the good ones are taken, they pursue unavailable men who possess the qualities they're looking for. Another cause for disloyalty amongst women is due to internalized self-hatred and low self esteem.

Women's inability to see value in themselves often causes them to act out in ways that are destructive to all parties involved. These are women who actually sleep with their friends' boyfriends and husbands. They purposely sleep with their girlfriend's significant other to prove to themselves that they are just as good, powerful and desirable as the other woman. Sometimes the malicious act often has more to do with the other woman than her man.

One of the worst things a woman can do to another woman is sleep with her man. It's actually a form of rape and emotional exploitation when you take from someone else what belongs to them. It potentially destroys the relationship with the couple. It serves to fuel the riff, disunity and competition between women. It also negatively affects the woman who operates as the mistress in the long run.

Too many women no longer respect a wedding ring on a man's finger. Their attitude is 'she wasn't making him happy anyway. So why can't I be happy? I make him happy.' As selfish as that sounds many women are out for what they can get and if that means another woman's husband, then so be it. If this shocks some of you, don't let it. There is a new breed of women out there today. Many have become tougher in the business world, and as they are used to getting what they want in the office, they now think that they can simply get any man they want too.

Female emancipation and sexual freedom have led many women to believe that they can go after what they want – including any man – regardless of his availability. And women are hurting other women in the process. The following story proves the cyclical damage that is being done.

Jenny was 45 years old with two teenage sons when she was recently left by her husband, a property developer, after 18 years of marriage for a woman 15 years younger than her. Naturally, she was heartbroken and grieved for her marriage. However, after several months, when the emotional scars began to heal, what emerged was a much tougher woman. Though she had suffered at the hands of a predatory female, she was beginning to realize that she was willing to behave in the same manner if it meant she could be happy again. In the past she would have simply ruled out having a relationship with a married man, but all that changed after another woman took her husband.

For the last few months, she, herself has been having an affair with a married man. What happened to her served to make her more single-minded in her pursuit of her wants. She boldly stated "I no longer believe in any sort of sisterhood. A woman has betrayed me and sadly I don't feel any loyalty to other women anymore. I used to believe in the sanctity of marriage but not any more."

Sadly, Jenny is not alone. More and more women are becoming cold and callous as they experience relational betrayal in their own lives. But, beyond the pursuit of a man, women suffer from many social and cultural issues that often put them at odds with one another.

Mirror, Mirror, On The Wall

Have you taken a look in the mirror lately? Oh yeah, what did you see? Did you see yourself for who you really are or for what society has taught you to believe about yourself? Women of all nationalities deal with anxieties concerning their appearance and body type. However, people of color struggle with this issue in a very unique way. Black women in America have always been measured by an imposed White (European) standard of beauty.

It is a standard that tells you what you are supposed to look like. If you both represent and embrace the standard it can offer a false sense of superiority and acceptance in a world that views you as an 'other'. If you don't represent the standard you may be negatively looked upon by society, as well as, many of your own people.

It is a standard that has caused countless White women to dye their hair blond, become super thin and enhance their breast size in order to resemble glorified media images. It is a standard that has caused many Asian women to undergo eye operations to widen their eyes in order to make them less narrow. It is a standard that has caused countless Indians to use skin lightening creams to appear fair.

I recently viewed a commercial typically shown in India. It almost knocked me off my seat. Two women walk through an airport from different directions. They recognize each other from a distance and quickly greet one another. One woman notices the other woman's dark complexion and hands her a jar of '9X'. The woman applies it to her face and she instantly turns white with European features. While she goes through her nine-second transformation a harp begins to gently play in the background. The once frazzled dark-skinned Indian woman jovially walks through the airport with a new complexion, new features and a new attitude. The commercial was selling skin lighting crème.

As disturbing as that commercial was, nothing could top a particular episode of *The Montel Williams Show* which featured a young Black woman who obviously was a poster-child for self-hatred. On the show she boldly stated, "I don't like dark-skin because it looks dirty to me. I do not like the big nose. I do not like the big lips. When I look at a Black person with a big nose they look like monkeys. Basically, society has categorized me as being Black. I don't want to be Black. Being born Black has been a curse...I like light-skin better. I feel it's more beautiful. "

Unfortunately, we live in a society where beauty has been racialized and used as a weapon against those who don't fit the bill. In our attempt to become beautiful, many of us have unconsciously viewed ourselves through the eyes of the dominant culture and their worship of White beauty. Some of us have even embraced what the White community views as beauty within our own community. Unfortunately, this has affected how we view our own complexions, hair, physical features and body type.

Who could forget the 1988 musical-drama film *School Daze* written and directed by Spike Lee? Based in part on Spike Lee's experiences at Atlanta's Morehouse College, it is a story about fraternity and sorority members clashing with other students at a historically Black college during homecoming weekend. Throughout the film, the Gamma Rays, also known as the Wannabes, battle it out in a fantasy dis-fest with a number of fellow co-eds known as the Jigaboos. The Wannabes were depicted as the pretty, light-skinned, long-haired, economically well-off women, while the Jigaboos were the dark-skinned, militant, politically and socially conscious women.

The dance performance scene from the movie perfectly displayed the tensions that always have and continue to exist amongst groups of women in the Black community such as: light-skin vs. dark-skin, good hair vs. bad hair, body type and a list of other social and cultural self-esteem issues. Each issue is unique in its own right and carries its own set of challenges.

Often times the treatment that women exhibit towards one another is rooted in a 'self-hatred' or negative feeling they often have for themselves. Whether too light, too dark, too fat, too skinny, too kinky, or too straight, many Black women have grown up with cultural insecurities and self-esteem issues created by White standards of beauty that are perpetuated by others within their own race and gender.

Depending upon one's overall physical make-up, the challenges that they endure may differ. Erica Lewis, an African American fitness instructor, shared her challenges growing up Black and female as a young child in her community.

Why We Hate Black Women

Erica's pain began at the age of seven when she was told she couldn't participate in the school's ballet recital because she exceeded the maximum weight requirement of 99lbs. After several weeks of group rehearsals and private practice, Erica was told on the day of the event that she was disqualified for being one pound too heavy. She was the only student in her entire class who couldn't be in the show. That was a day she would never forget.

By the time Erica turned 10 years old, she was known as 'Fat, Black and Ugly Erica'. Dark skin was not in fashion during those times. In fact, she was often made a target because of her complexion. Kids would run behind her and wipe her neck with tissue just to see if she was really that dark or if her neck was dirty.

Once in middle school, things went from bad to worse. Not only was her dark-skin a burden, but the combination of a mouth full of braces and a drippy jheri curl put her at odds with everyone. Teachers would always tell her, "You gotta pretty face, if you just lost some weight." The comments, ridicule and insensitive treatment drove her to several fad diets which caused her to lose the weight just to gain it back again. Regardless of how much weight she lost she still saw herself as 'Fat, Black, and Ugly Erica' with the jheri curl and braces.

By time she was in the 10th grade, Erica had a crush on a cute dark-skinned boy in her school. When the possibility of them dating came up he told her 'You're cute but you're too dark and if you were just lighter you would be prettier.' Meanwhile, all of her light-skinned friends had boyfriends. The sharp contrast in their realities created both an envy and hatred in her heart for her light-skinned friends. They possessed a trait that she was penalized for not having.

Erica quickly realized that being dark wasn't getting her anywhere. So, she asked a classmate who was lighter than her what she did to keep her skin so light because everyday she seemed so bright. She replied, "BLEACH." Little did Erica know that the girl actually used concealer. However, all she could think of was the word 'bleach.'

After school Erica ran home and poured Clorox in the sink and began to scrub her face with bleach. The smell was awful but she was determined to lighten her skin if it was the last thing she did. Luckily, her mother could smell it from the back of the house and got to her in enough time to keep her from damaging her skin. She immediately made her drain the sink along with the idea of becoming lighter with bleach. At that time, all Erica experienced was her hope of dating that boy slowly draining down the sink. The saga of insecurity and low self-worth lingered on for several years after that adolescent experience.

At age 24 Erica met the guy that she thought would become her husband. But what he turned out to be was the experience that changed her life. They shared a 2 year relationship that initiated the healing process that Erica so desperately needed. It was he who gave her the FIRST compliment about her complexion that she ever received.

In a moment of complete emotional transparency he revealed to her that she had the prettiest skin he'd ever seen. Even though the relationship did not last, their time together helped her move beyond her self-destructive behavior about her skin and body. Wow, who would've thought that one compliment could wipe out an entire childhood of pain, hurt and deeply imbedded insecurities about one's skin tone.

Unfortunately, Erica is not alone. There are many women who suffer from issues of weight, complexion, hair and body type which sometimes create enormous amounts of dissension amongst Black women. Jealousy and self-imposed insecurities often fertilize the ground from which all tension is spewed amongst women. Rather than Erica entering into confrontations with other women, she instead engaged in self-inflicted abuse by overeating.

However, if you were to randomly ask any Black woman if they have ever had an issue of contention with another female in their life I can assure you the answer would emphatically be yes. During interviews for this book, women from across the nation anxiously shared their stories of struggles which often stem back to childhood.

Why We Hate Black Women

Many women have described being picked on, being beaten up or jumped by other females, having their hair ripped out, having their face scarred, having their clothes destroyed, having their jewelry broken or stolen, being gossiped about, being lied on and experiencing a host of other cruel things just because someone didn't like them. Some were singled out because of their appearance, complexion, length of hair, clothing fashion and the like.

There are women, on the other hand, who gossip, make snide remarks, give evil looks and cat-fight! They may size each other up for the labels they are or are not wearing, the job title they should or should not have, the bag that is or is not real, the hair that is or really is not theirs, and the clothes that do or do not properly fit. It just doesn't stop.

Rather than complimenting a woman on how nice she looks, some will enter into a trance staring at the crown or part in another woman's head trying to figure out if the hair is real. The same is true for the need to stare at another woman's blouse to determine if it is authentic or not. How about the necessity to always have something to say no matter how cutting and cynical it may be? Growing up Black and female has definitely presented challenges for some.

During my interview process I came across countless women who shared their personal feelings and experiences growing up.

"I constantly have random broads eye-ballin' me for no good reason every time I go out. I could just hear them now. Saying things like 'Look at her outfit.' 'Where does she think she's going lookin' all cute?' 'Why she look so darn happy?' 'She ain't even all that.' Why do we have to roll our eyes every time we see someone who's pretty? Why do we have to find a reason to roll our eyes and say something negative? This so-called sisterhood thing is dead."

Janette, 27, Bank Teller

"For as long as I can remember I have always had to prove my 'blackness' to anyone who questioned my roots because of my fair

134

skin and green eyes. Over the years I also witnessed my mother suffer because of her complexion. She lost friends and was often falsely blamed for thinking she was superior. Being light skinned was pure hell."

Shawnte, 31, Educator

"I remember when I was about 4 or 5, sitting in my rocking chair in the kitchen. My mom looked at me and told me to squeeze my nose. I realized not too long after that she was trying to keep my nose from spreading like hers."

Jewel, 32, Software Sales

"People often look at me and assume that my life is perfect because of my appearance. I'm biracial but I look like a white woman. I have had problems my whole life with other women, especially those who look differently from myself. I've been in abusive relationships with dark-skinned black men who only viewed me as a "trophy slut" because of how I looked. I have difficulty trusting anyone with darker skin because of how I have been treated."

Melinda 46, Photographer

"I have had another sister hate on me for no reason without knowing me, never really cared [to] ask her but sisterhood went down the drain and the hating started when most found that men preferred one kind of girl over another...well at least that's what I think...and yes I have a little thing against skinny chicks...but there's no competition because guys want what they see in XXL not vogue... thick is always going to be "eye candy."

Keisha, 23, Student

As you can see, the reasons women often hate on one another differ. Whether due to insecurities, cultural self-esteem issues, the vestiges of slavery or just plain envy, sisterhood amongst Black women needs to be refortified. If more women took the time to create a welcoming atmosphere of open and honest dialogue, they could develop a greater level of empathy for one another.

Chapter 8

Why Black Men Don't Want You

oreign women are more willing to stand by their man through thick and through thin. When I fight with my wife she still makes me my favorite dinner and irons my clothes. And that's not being weak. That's making a decision to be strong in bad times. And it's not that I didn't want a Black woman but I like my women like I like my beer, imported. It doesn't give you a headache the next day like American beer because they spend more time making it.

James, Mortgage Broker, Philadelphia, PA

~~~~~

I date only White women because Black women are trifling, loud and rude. They give us too much grief. They come with so much baggage. It's just too much work. They're just extra. They are materialistic and gold diggers. The only Black woman I deal with is my mother.

<div align="right">

Bruce, Bill Collector, Phoenix, Arizona

</div>

~~~~~

Black women have issues and they typically rationalize those issues away. There is a subculture among our women in which they engage in self-justifying behavior. Therefore, they have a good reason to verbally abuse us, cheat on us, emasculate us and whatever else they decide to do. So, if a wife decides she doesn't want to have sex with her husband, her girlfriends will enable her behavior instead of challenging her. They want us to change but we're forced to accept them for who and how they are. Both of us must go through a process of growth and development. So, why is it ok for their development to be arrested but our development has to continue?

Robert, Educator, New Jersey

No other women on the face of the earth have been as abandoned, rejected and betrayed by their own men as have Black women in America. Rather than protecting and defending them, many have exposed them before the entire world and have hung them out to dry. No matter where you turn you can find a Black man who will unapologetically broadcast his disgust and long list of reasons for choosing to date outside his race.

Television talk shows, blog posts, magazine articles, talk radio and YouTube videos are ripe with men who have devalued Black women.

While many bitter men spew ignorance across television and radio airwaves, others raise legitimate concerns that must be further examined. However, the verbal attack on Black women has been so damaging that members outside of our own community have joined in on the verbal assault.

Several years ago *Sister 2 Sister Magazine* published a 'letter to the editor' written by a White woman whose comments ignited a fury amongst Black men and women. The following is the anonymous woman's comments:

Dear Jamie,

I'm sorry but I would like to challenge some of your Black male readers.

I am a White female who is engaged to a Black male--good-looking, educated and loving. I just don't understand a lot of Black females' attitudes about our relationship. My man decided he wanted me because the pickings amongst Black women were slim to none. As he said they were either too fat, too loud, too mean, too argumentative, too needy, too materialistic or carrying too much excess baggage.

Before I became engaged, whenever I went out I was constantly approached by Black men, willing to wine and dine me and give me the world. If Black women are so up in arms about us being with their men, why don't they look at themselves and make some changes. I am tired of the dirty looks I get and snide remarks when we're out in public.

I would like to hear from some Black men about why we are so appealing and coveted by them. Bryant Gumble just left his wife of 26 years for one of us. Charles Barkley, Scottie Pippen, the model Tyson Beckford, Montell Williams, Quincy Jones, James Earl Jones, Harry Belafonte, Sydney Poitier, Kofi Anan, Cuba Gooding Jr., Don Cornelius, Berry Gordy, Billy Blanks, Larry Fishburne, Wesley Snipes...I could go on and on.

But right now I'm a little angry and that is why I wrote this so hurriedly. Don't be mad with us White women because so many of your men want us. Get your acts together and <u>learn from us and we may lead you to treat your men better</u>. If I'm wrong, Black men, let me know.

At the time of the article's release, it opened up a racial/relational pandora's box of issues that have yet to be resolved. While some Black men and women were angry over her letter, others were relieved that someone finally spoke up. Interestingly, when I share this letter with audiences across the nation, I generally get emotionally-charged intellectual responses. In other words, they are intellectual responses seasoned with emotion or vice versa.

When sistahs explain why they believe Black men leave them for White women, generally speaking, both the White woman and Black man are to blame. In fact, it is common to hear responses such as:

- White women have low self-esteem
- White women are passive, easy to manipulate, and can be run over
- White women are nasty and will give it up too easily (sex)
- White women take abuse and will do anything to keep a Black man
- White women are still considered trophies in society

139

- Black men are lazy and don't want to work for anything (a relationship)
- Black men don't want to be challenged to be better
- Black men just want to do what they want to do and not be held accountable for their actions
- Black men are sell-outs and ashamed of their race
- Black men are too weak to deal with a real sistah

Sometimes, along with these responses comes a romanticized list of attributes explaining how fabulous Black women are and how some Black men are just too dumb to see it. While some take an introspective look at themselves, others hold a wide-spread belief that as Black women, they've got it all together. The problem is Black women have been so demonized, vilified, and disrespected throughout time that some overcompensate by presenting grandiose depictions of Black women when defending themselves.

Meanwhile, other women whom I've encountered have acknowledged and agreed in part with the overall critical assessment of Black women. They recognize the validity of such statements though they do not embrace the tone in which the criticisms are given.

As chilling as the *Sister 2 Sister* letter to the editor was, the most controversial statement was made towards the end. After explaining how difficult Black women are, she ended with the following statement, "learn from us and we may lead you to treat your men better." Wow, what a bold and violently provocative statement.

At first glance, I lumped her statement in with the rest of the letter. But, after reading the letter in further detail I isolated the statement from the rest of the passage for further consideration. I then conducted an informal survey to see what Black women thought about that statement. I posed the following question. "If a White woman taught a class, wrote a book or conducted a seminar on How To Attract & Keep A Good Black Man: 10 Secrets Every

Black Woman Wishes She Knew would you be willing to be instructed by her?"

As you can already imagine, the majority of Black women emphatically said "H-E-L-L NO!" In fact, most of the women surveyed used more colorful and descriptive language (expletives) to express their feelings. Just the thought of a White woman trying to tell them how to secure a relationship with a Black man aggravated the majority of those surveyed. Interestingly, at least some women were open to taking the class if taught by a Black man.

Why Are So Many Black Men Leaving Black Women?

The percentages of Black men and women dating outside their races have increased significantly over the last decade. More so now than ever before, it has become common to see a Black man with a White woman (or non-African American) on his arm.

The general belief was that the more successful a Black man became, the more likely it was that he would select a White woman as his companion.

The reality, however, proves that socioeconomic levels have little to do with the dating selection process. In fact, there are more cases of lower-income Black men selecting White women than those at the top. The ultimate question is, "Why are so many Black women abandoned by Black men?" The search for the answer to this question became one of my main motivations for writing this book.

My research has concluded that the majority of Black men that I've both interviewed and studied have made an exclusive allegiance towards Black women. They have neither dated nor married non-Black women. As with all ethnic and racial groups, most men and women marry within their own culture. However, a growing number of Black men are choosing to leave sistahs behind in pursuit of something all together different.

Why We Hate Black Women

It is important to note that there are Black men who have dated and/or married non-Black women as a result of a genuine love interest. They simply met, connected and fell in love with a woman outside of their cultural experience. On the other hand, there are others who have made an intentional decision to collectively leave all Black women alone in exchange for 'the alternative.

While an incalculable number of reasons have been cited to justify why men have dismissed Black women as a legitimate dating option, they all fit within four (4) major categories.

Reason #1: Lack of Racial Solidarity

Generally speaking, Black men don't have the same level of racial solidarity that Black women are known for having. When it comes to matters of the heart or sexual pleasure, men are more willing to explore their options across cultural lines than are Black women. This is due, in part, to the number of dating options men have available to them.

It is not uncommon for a Black man to be seen partnered with a White, Latin or Asian woman. However, Black women are the least likely to date/marry outside of their race.

Why? A considerable number of young girls have been taught and raised to find a 'Good Black Man.' In fact, many were warned against bringing a White boy home to their parent's doorstep. The dark sexual history between Black women and White men has significantly contributed to the discouragement of interracial dating.

Black women's upbringing has caused many to have disdain for interracial dating. A lot of sistahs simply can't stand to see brothers with White women on their arms. It's mainly because Black women view Black men's transition across cultural lines as the ultimate slap in the face and rejection of African-American women. This belief often creates resentment and bitterness in the hearts of many women.

Chapter 8: Why Black Men Don't Want You

Do I like seeing Black men with White women? No! Do I like seeing Black women with White men? No! Honestly, I do feel a pang of betrayal when I see it. I want to say, "All of these beautiful African queens and you want that? All these beautiful strong African kings and you wanted that?" But people are grown and make their own choices. That's not a choice that I can make because I LOVE Black men. The spiritual connection, their energy, the strength in the melanin, our souls working and soaring to the same beat of the drum. The Caucasian doesn't hear the drum or feel it. Angie Stone said it best, "Black brother, strong brother, there is no one above you. I hope that you know that I'm here for you...."
Jamie, 34, Technician

In the 2001 movie, *The Brothers*, comedy-actor Bill Bellamy's character, Brian Palmer, had an exchange with his mother Helen about how his father left her for a White woman. The dialogue was humorous, but it may reflect an inside perspective on how sistahs feel about their men leaving them for 'the alternative' (Asian/White/Latin women). The dialogue goes as follows:

Mom: Oh don't bring up that fool again. He left me for
     some White woman.
Son: She's Hawaiian.
Mom: If she ain't Black, she's White.
Son: See, that's what I'm talkin' about mama. That's
     just ridiculous.
Mom: Facts of life.
Son: That's crazy...Latino women?
Mom: A White woman with a taco.
Son: Oh so I just guess Asian woman...
Mom: A White woman who don't speaka the God--mn
     English.

Often times, women ask the question: "Why do you date outside your race?" Men respond by asking: "Why do Black women think they own Black men?"or "Why do they think we owe them something?" I personally think these are good questions that deserve even better answers.

143

First, it is true. Black women do not own Black men. There is no legal document obligating Black men to remain exclusively with Black women. And honestly, I don't think Black women want to force Black men to commit. They want Black men to want to commit. They want to be wanted, desired and chosen by good Black men.

So, Black women don't want ownership of Black men. However, what they do want is for Black men to own up to their responsibilities as men, husbands and fathers. As we have described elsewhere in this book, Black women are known for having unrealistic expectations with men. And in some cases it's true. However, Black women have every right to expect their men to love them unconditionally, maintain sexual integrity, raise their children, and provide for their family. These aren't unreasonable requests. They are simply things that go along with being in a relationship.

Second, Black men do owe Black women something. When you look at the hard-core facts, 42.3% of Black women have never been married and 70% of Black households are run by single parent women. By and large, this is due to the fact that Black men are not committing to Black women. As a result, families are breaking down and communities are being destroyed. So, do we owe Black women something? Yes we do.

We owe Black women our allegiance. We owe them an opportunity to experience the best of who we are. We owe them the right to love and happiness. We owe them the chance of having dreams of a successful marriage and family fulfilled. We owe them an apology for all the hurt and pain that we put them through. Even if we weren't responsible for their pain, we can participate in their healing. We owe them our lives.

It's time for Black men to sport a little racial solidarity. It simply means to unite and maintain harmony. Make a commitment to date Black women until you find the one who fits the best. If you come across a triflin' sistah, move on until you find what you're looking for. But don't abandon ship and give up on all sisters. After all that Black men have put them through, the majority of them have not given up on us, so why should we give up on them?

Reason #2: Cultural Stereotypes

While conducting research for the book I came across a blog titled *"The Top Ten Reasons Why It's Hard To Date A Black Woman"* by Matthew Lynch. The objective of the article was to illustrate issues relating to Black men's interaction, or lack thereof, with Black women. He interviewed a small cross-section of men and generated a list of 50 reasons why Black men find it hard to date Black women. The following list details the top 10 reasons on his list.

1. Black women make Black men feel under-appreciated, unwarranted and irresponsible and regressive.
2. Black women are too aggressive and no longer patient in waiting on the pursuit of a man.
3. Black women are strong headed, too independent which presents great challenges in relationships
4. Black women are masculine in that they are controlling and like to run the relationship.
5. Black women expect too much. They are gold diggers who will not look twice at a blue collar Black man.
6. Black women are hot headed and have bad attitudes
7. Black women stop caring about their appearance after a certain age
8. Black women are not as sexually open as other races, especially in regards to oral sex
9. Black women's tolerance is far too low; they are no longer empathetic to the Black man's struggle in White America
10. Black women do not cater to their men

Now, if you are like most women I've shared this list with, you are probably pissed off, offended, and ready to verbally slay someone right about now. While surveying Black women's response to this list, this is what they had to say:

145

Why We Hate Black Women

"Not all Black women are men hating, obese, low class hoochies. And stop putting other races on a freaking pedestal. There are plenty of ignorant, out of shape, classless White/Hispanic/Asian women in the world. You all just choose to turn a blind eye to their shortcomings. Shake off the mental chains. White ain't always right. And if you don't believe me just go to Wal-Mart on any given day, I've never seen so many ugly, lumpy, crass looking women of all races in my life. It's not just sisters with stank attitudes, but somehow we're the only ones that get a bad rap."

Dawn, 45, Sales

One of the reasons why I believe women of other races are taking Black men is because of the way they were raised. Black girls in specific neighborhoods and in single parent homes often see their mothers go from man to man. One man for this bill, one man for that bill, etc. Never taking care of themselves or being self-sufficient or efficient as a single woman handling her business which spills over into the daughters looking for the dude to take care of them.

Quamara, 41, Manager

"They say they choose White women because we are too loud and have too much attitude. They call us materialistic and judgmental. They complain about our fake nails and fake hair and heavier frames. They say we never want to please them in bed and hate giving oral sex. In other words, they feel like we aren't worth the effort and deem us less than. So, not only do we have to look at their image when we're told what's beautiful but we have to listen to all these so-called qualities that make us even less attractive.

Tash, 29, Administrator

Black men are dating outside their race...and they have an issue with Black women and the attitude stigmas...I've been confused about it, but now it's clear. When a man has grown up under the iron fist of his mother, grandmother and sisters yelling, screaming, _hollering and acting like wild kingdom they are turned off from the attitude of Black women from conception, birth, and adolescence into maturity. Children always look at their parents and say what they will do differently when they grow up and when a male child has to hear all of the above mentioned go on for his entire life, he REFUSES to go through it in a romantic relationship; hence his crossing over to what appears to be greener pastures. What a shame._

Erica, 36, Fitness Instructor

Before you start shoutin' 'Amen' from every rooftop, let's keep one thing in mind. This list is absolutely true. This list is also absolutely false. See, there are numerous women who represent this list in its entirety. Then there are women who represent elements of this list, whether conscious of it or not. Finally, there are women who don't have a thread of commonality with anything on this list.

In all reality, the list should be offensive to both Black women and Black men alike. Why? It is an unfair indictment of all Black women which further perpetuates the already skewed perception that people have of Black women.

This list is no more absolute than the generalized negative classification of Black men. You've heard it all before. A sistah who is frustrated with Black men will say, "There ain't no good Black men out there. They are either on drugs, in gangs, in jail, gay, dead or with White women. The rest are liars, cheaters and are only interested in one thing, sex." As offensive as the previous list is to Black women, so are these statements to Black men.

As long we continue to view each other through these culturally skewed, stereotypical lenses, we will never close the ever-increasing love gap between Black men and Black women. Rather, it will cause more men to embrace the ethnic alternative: White women. Although most Black men choose to date Black women, many Black men make the claim that Black women are just too difficult to deal with. They state that White women are easier to get. Meaning, the effort one has to put into getting a

Why We Hate Black Women

Black girl's attention is cut in half when dealing with a White woman. In many cases, this statement is absolutely true.

The reason White women are probably easier to deal with is because most of them don't have a personal history of pain, rejection, abuse, and betrayal from scores of Black men. While some sistahs give men the third-degree, White women often enter into relationships with Black men with their eyes wide shut. They have no suspicions because they have no reason to. There's no past record of offense that would cause them to be suspicious. One sistah said it quite simply.

Intelligent, confident, and secure Black women have been labeled as "high maintenance," and it's true. We are extremely selective; we don't lavish a man with our gifts until we are convinced he deserves them. We are more challenging; we require more time, effort, and creativity. Quite often, we end up "alone" because a brother will choose a woman who doesn't require much from him; and he settles for what is easy and convenient. And brothers, just admit it - some of you simply don't want to work that hard. You want the benefits of having a Mercedes, by putting forth the effort required of a Yugo. Many brothers want the perks without the responsibilities. They don't want to take the time to cultivate the basics that must be established before any workable, mature, rewarding relationship can grow.

Natasha, 37, Accountant

"This entire situation boils down to the fact that Black men are jumping to various races of women because they don't want to deal with the mess they've created with Black women. They'd rather date outside of their race because the mess that exists in the Black world ain't in the Spanish or White world. It looks like a clean slate...but all they are doing is transferring the mess. Meanwhile we are cleaning up their mess by raising babies alone, digging our way out of debt, and healing from their all of their lies and broken promises, etc.

Erica, 36, Fitness Instructor

For the record, I want to dispel one of the greatest lies held against Black men – that we date White women to gain a trophy. It's about being happy. I don't have time to come home to the ongoing battles waged by many women toward their men. Brothers are now saying, I can go in another direction and not have to deal with all the headaches. But Black women see it as a trophy thing. They refuse to see their role in why Black men date outside of the race.

John, 48, Executive

Reason #3: Sexual Fulfillment

Historically, Black women have always been considered the pinnacle of sexuality. From plantation rooted stereotypes to modern day imagery, Black women have been falsely depicted as erotic freaks with an insatiable desire for sex. However, when you speak to many brothers, they will profess the exact opposite. In fact, they believe Black women in general have lots of sexual hang-ups that keep them from fully exploring their sexuality.

Religious beliefs, traditional thinking, child molestation, abuse, rape, historical and modern day sexual stereotypes and a whole host of other contributing factors often play into some Black women's sexual choices. Men, on the other hand, are very sexually driven and often base their decisions on their penis and an erection. Their preoccupation with sex and personal gratification has caused them to seek fulfillment wherever it may be found. Race, culture and ethnicity are often least on their minds when concerning sex. The motto 'we're all dark when the lights go out' is the justification used to explore women of all cultures.

It is widely believed by men that Black women are not as sexually adventurous as White, Asian and Latino women. In essence, Black women generally aren't as willing to crack their legs open or drop to their knees as quickly or as frequently as other women. So, Black men's desires coupled with Black women's supposed unwillingness to sexually perform have created sexual incompatibility; this in turn has caused men to drift off to other cultures of women.

Why We Hate Black Women

Research does indicate that Black women's sexual practices are generally more conservative than those of White women. In *Stolen Women: Reclaiming Our Sexuality, Taking Back Our Lives*, Gail E. Wyatt shares her findings from her in-depth research with samples of women in Los Angeles County. She found that while Black women were slightly more likely than White women to have an extramarital affair, White women tended to have more sexual relationships during adolescence, were more likely to initiate sex with their partner, were more likely to engage in cunnilingus, fellatio, and anal sex, and were more likely to engage in sex with more than one person at a time.

These findings are in no way being used as a criticism to either Black or White women, but rather to point out that the long held stereotype of Black women as oversexed and promiscuous is unfounded and that the notion of sexual conservativism among Black women has merit.

Truth be told, one of the main culprits behind men's desire to sexually explore other women is their indulgence in pornography. Men's sexual fantasies and expectations have become increasingly shaped by the standards of porn. Their expectations of how a woman should look and behave are made unrealistic through their consumption of the images portrayed in pornography. Porn teaches men to view women as objects rather than human beings. And they look for the attributes in women that they see in porn: big breasts, blonde hair, and curvier bodies. One male admitted:

"This whole interest in dating outside our race, I believe comes from pornography. I was exposed to pornography at the age of twelve years old accidently. In the bathroom at my grandmother's house, my uncle had a stack of porno magazines. And with all of the images, not one of them was a sistah. So, as a young Black man I grew up with the visions subconsciously, so as I got older and started finding those women who were attracted to me I gravitated towards those types of women."

Chapter 8: Why Black Men Don't Want You

Often, Black men's voyeuristic fetish has led from Black porn to White porn, Asian porn, and Latin porn as well. Not only did the pornography feed their addiction for sex, it created a curiosity for those women as well. Because porn is typically about male gratification, it's always a woman sexually satisfying a man whether it be vaginal, anal or oral penetration, especially oral penetration. That's why so many men push for oral sex all the time, even if the woman's not interested. Because it is so frequently done in porn, it is naturally expected in real relationships as well. And if a woman does not accommodate his request, she is often dismissed for the one who will indulge. When I spoke to Black women about them not being as sexually open as women from other cultures, especially concerning oral sex, one single Black woman responded with the following statement.

"It is amazing to me how oral sex plays such a large part in their masculinity. For a woman to fall down on her knees, wrap her lips around his penis and bring him to this exclamation point of pleasure seems to be the height of his career. It seems to be his primary goal and emphasis in life. It's ridiculous. He uses that woman's lips as a length of measuring: measuring his penis, measuring his status, and the more lips he has wrapped around his penis, the longer his penis gets, the longer his status gets, the longer the stories get, over him having a beer with the friends. And so on and so on. He uses the mouths of women to measure who he is because of his other insecurities in life. He's using oral sex as his means of success."

Erica, 36, Fitness Instructor

Another sister said:

"We are extremely selective; we don't lavish a man with our gifts until we are convinced he deserves them. We are more challenging; we require more time, effort, and creativity. Quite

151

often, we end up "alone" because a brother will choose a woman who doesn't require much from him; and he settles for what is easy and convenient...Many brothers want the perks without the responsibilities. They don't want to take the time to cultivate the basics that must be established before any workable, mature, rewarding relationship can grow."

Teresa, 42, Heathcare Administrator

"That's right. Blame the woman Adam. Blame the woman. God still holds you responsible for having no backbone! You know the main reason you want White women is for immoral and unnatural sex. You probably blame Black women for the men who want other men too! It's ridiculous! All Black men who claim the Black woman has made them turn to White women – hog wash! You have no substance; you have no character; you have no strength! This is what White America has done to you. You are shiftless, vain, characterless and you are racist. Whatever happened to Dr. King's message – "Judge people by the content of their character, not the color of their skin!" What you are really judging women by is the perversion of their sex. Admit it. You want a long haired freak but you don't have the backbone to admit it."

Brenda, 39, Mortgage Processor

A Black male, Steve, who weighed in on the issues candidly said:

"Black chicks not in no more, man. They always demanding something from a brother. White and Latino girls are in now. White girls now got fat as@es. White girls don't have no attitudes. White girls give more sexual favors. White girls are easier and you get more for your money. Spanish girls are a step up from Black chicks. They have better skin tones, real hair and they are just sexier. Black women need to step up their competition."

Steve's comments are widely held by Black men of all ages, backgrounds, occupations, and financial levels. So, they sexually pursue White women because they're known for being sexually easy and willing to give good head at a moment's notice. They are known for being oral sex connoisseurs.

The attitudes of White females regarding oral sex are generally different than the attitudes of Black females. While Whites are free to talk about it with little to no embarrassment, Black women are usually less cooperative. So, when Black men are asked why they like dating White girls, they grab their crotches and smile. Meanwhile sisters are marginalized by these Black men as having no oral talent. So, sistahs are passed over because of their unwillingness to accommodate a man's sexual request as quickly or as often as he would like.

There are Black men who have a sexual craving for Latin women who are known for being passionately erotic, sensual and sexy. So, not only are Black women losing their men to White women but Latin women as well. In fact, Dominican and Brazilian women have become the new craze and Black men are traveling hundreds of miles to fulfill a sexual fantasy.

The Dominican Republic and, more importantly, Rio de Janeiro, Brazil have become known as the 'Black Man's Paradise'. It has become a sexual rite-of-passage for many African-American men. In fact, Brazilian women are stealing the hearts, minds and imaginations of Black men each and every day. In my travels I have personally met Black men who have made Rio, the Dominican Republic and other exotic hot spots their home away from home. They have found a certain kind of sex and freedom absent from their own relationships.

In these third-world countries Black men receive treatment unparallel to anywhere else. From the moment they step off the plane they are made objects of affection by beauties who provide a multitude of services. Sex is not the only thing for sale. Companionship is also available for purchase. Brazilian prostitutes are coveted around the world because they provide a 'Girlfriend Experience' unmatched by others.

Why We Hate Black Women

Brazilian women target three things: a man's eyes, his erotic desires and his ego. This three-prong attack is what keeps Black men coming back to Rio de Janeiro. First, Brazilian women have mastered the art of eye candy. It has been said that they rank among the most beautiful women on the planet.

Whether due to genetics or plastic surgery, they are known for having an African booty, a European face and a caramel complexion. The beauty these women possess have caused men to change the physical standard of what they consider attractive and desirable. Unfortunately, once many of these men make it back to the states their girlfriends and wives no longer fit the bill.

Second, Brazilian women target a man's erotic desires. Brazilian women are said to exceed a man's expectations with mind-blowing sex. For instance, interactions with Brazilian prostitutes last from several hours to several days. In fact, for a nominal fee of $35-$40 American dollars a man can do whatever he wants: vaginal, oral, and anal sex, ménage trois, urination, strangulation, and a host of other sexual acts typically not carried out by their significant others. So, it gives men an opportunity to do what they could never dare do with their partners.

Third, Brazilian women target a man's ego. More so than sex, the ego trip is what keeps Black men flying back and forth to Brazil. In most cases, men aren't traveling halfway across the country just for sex. You can get sex anywhere. Beyond the sexual fantasy is the treatment they receive.

Black men are made to feel like kings. These women meet an emotional need that creates a delusional feeling that the prostitute is a true partner in a relationship, however brief. In essence, they provide a Girlfriend Experience which is far different from a straightforward exchange of money for orgasm. The prostitute acts as if she cares for the client and enjoys her intimacy with him. She even pampers him in ways unmatched by his own woman.

When the sex is over, often the real service begins. These women are known to hug, kiss, and even rub and massage the backs and feet of their clients. They will clean up, do the laundry, run to the store, and even cook the food. They will compliment them and give them the kind of attention they could never get back home.

As a result, these prostitutes are of greater emotional importance to them than their relationships with their own wives and girlfriends. These men engage in social, courting behaviors that are flavored with degrees of romance. By the trip's end, some are tempted to leave their partners for good.

The problem with this entire scenario is that this transactional relationship is based upon a lie. These women are poor people from a third world country who use both their beauty and their body for profit. It's a business. Simply put, they're sex hustlers whose main objective is to get that money and they'll do whatever it takes to secure it.

Brazilian prostitutes are willing to sex, cook, clean, massage and pamper men for an entire day for only $35 - $40 bucks because they ultimately want to hit the jackpot. What they're really looking for is a financial commitment. They will either turn you out with mind-blowing sex, pamper you until you fall in love, or have sex without a condom in order to get pregnant and trap you with a green card baby.

The goal is to get as many American boyfriends as possible because if they each send $300-$400 a month, and you have five boyfriends, that's $1500 - $2000 that's coming every thirty days. But even with this newfound money, she will still go out to hustle because she knows that eventually the man will get tired of sending money each month and the source will dry up. So, she looks for someone new to replace the last guy.

When everything is all said and done, these Black men have done much more harm than good. Even though they receive the benefits of sex, the short and long-term implications of their actions are far more damaging. In addition to the financial toll that it plays in a person's life, it also creates relational and sexual frustration with his woman back at home. Why? It's simple.

These women are professional sex workers who have mastered the art of sexual pleasure and will perform any and every sexual act imaginable. They have paid for plastic surgery and stay in the gym all day to sculpt the perfect body. They wear the sexiest bathing suits, clothes and undergarments to entice their clients. They indulge in the most meticulous grooming to stimulate the senses. They pamper their clients by catering to their every need and desire. In essence, they create the perfect fantasy for Black men.

Now compare that to a real-life wife who has stretch marks from giving birth to children. They have occasional bad hair days, corns on their feet, and scars on the skin. They enter the bedroom with raggedy robes, sweat socks, girdles, hair rollers and doo-rags, and baggy draws. There are nights when they're too tired or just might not be in the mood.

The problem comes in when men expect their wives to be like the prostitute. No, they don't want their partners to be a prostitute but they want them to look like her, be fit like her, perform like her, and desire it as much as her. When he gets none of the above, he becomes frustrated because his reality doesn't compare to the lie that the prostitute created for him.

Reason #4: The Relational Empowerment Struggle

Through my personal observation and research I have found another dynamic that has contributed to the pandemic of unpartnered Black women. As some Black women seek to empower themselves, their personal lives suffer. In fact, with each new level of accomplishment, it seems that they succeed in further shrinking the dating pool of available men.

I recently watched a discussion concerning the struggles of "Strong Black Women" that took place during an episode of the *Tyra Bank Show*. The discussion featured a focus group comprised of men and women of White, Asian, Latin, and Black heritages. A young Black twenty-something female burst out in tears as she revealed her personal plight in the dating scene. The young lady appeared in pain as she said:

"Nobody seems to understand how hard it is for a Black woman. I'm educated. I was always raised to take care of myself because if

a Black man didn't want me then I would still have to be able to raise my kids or take care of myself. But what hurts so much is that even after accomplishing all of this Black men don't want me. White men don't want me. Asian men don't want me. Latin men don't want me. And it's so discouraging."

Black women are being forced to make an unfair choice. Either pursue your mission or a man. It is a decision that no one should be forced to make. Every woman should be privileged enough to have the best of both worlds. Unfortunately, we're seeing the opposite take place.

There are four types of women who have succeeded in personally empowering themselves. However, it has had a negative impact on their relationships. Consider the scenarios of the following four types of women.

I. College Women Educate Themselves Out Of A Man

On most predominately White college and university campuses across the nation, there are more enrolled Black women than Black men. Therefore, the first major strike against Black women is the male/female ratio. The men are significantly outnumbered giving them an unlimited supply of dating options across all ethnic and racial lines. In other words, Black women are not only in competition with themselves, but with their White, Asian and Latina female counterparts as well.

While there are Black men who remain committed to Black women, an overwhelming number of Black men on college campuses choose not to date Black women at all. They may sex them, but many do not enter into meaningful relationships with them. So, there are an alarming number of Black women in college who are single or forced to pursue off-campus romantic relationships.

The second challenge women face is the competitive relationship between the sexes. While they all start off on an equal playing field, it seldom ends that way. With both in pursuit of similar goals of attainment (education, degrees, and employment), they often subconsciously compete with one another rather than collaborate. While Black men struggle with poor retention rates, Black women often cross the finish line with their B.A., B.S., M.A., M.B.A, Ph.D. and J.D. degrees.

It has been stated that White women graduate school with their M.R.S. (Mrs.) degree. In addition to their education, they often find a mate within or shortly after their college experience. However, Black women generally have a very different outcome which leads to the third dilemma.

More Black women than Black men have achieved the higher levels of educational attainment that position individuals for better employment and higher salaries. Their male counterparts, on the other hand, may face challenges in life that are associated with their lower levels of achievement in education. Ultimately, this dynamic negatively affects the relationship status of Black college women. As a result, many live a single life.

II. Corporate Women Employ Themselves Out Of A Man

We are all familiar with this woman. This is a woman who has landed a great job, works hard, and earns a decent to comfortable salary. Her profile (whether entry level or executive) typically reflects a self-sufficient lifestyle. She, most likely, has her own residence, car, benefits, personal savings, investments and possibly the ability to buy and/or travel whenever she may well please.

However, once she enters the workforce her career places her in a working environment with a limited number of available Black men to choose from. The men who are employed within a corporate setting generally fall into one of three categories.

They are either: 1) the unavailable Black man who is currently married or in a committed relationship, 2) the single professional Black man who thinks he's God's gift to women because he's got a good job. Depending upon the male, he may come across as arrogant, chauvinistic, or even playa-like because he knows he's a hot commodity in the dating world and 3) the available but undesirable Black man who may either make considerably less money or he represents the 'nice guy' type who lacks an element of swag (confidence, charisma, assertiveness with women, fashion, etc.). With so few options, it becomes increasingly difficult to secure a quality relationship. She, therefore, remains alone.

III. Community Women Mobilize Themselves Out Of A Man
Now, this is a woman who is on the move. She's an organizer. She can motivate the hopeless, mobilize the fragmented and mortify the enemy. Her life is dedicated to the cause of enhancing the quality of life for her people. She can raise funds for community causes, educate people on issues that affect the community and lead the charge against oppression on all fronts.

She's a freedom fighter who will stick her own neck out on the line for justice and equality. She will march to the capital, participate in rallies, write letters to public officials and participate in civil disobedient demonstrations that address the causes that she's so passionate about. She's ride or die when it comes to the freedom of her people. Yet, her cultural commitment to the race has left her all by her lonesome.

IV. Church Women Spiritualize Themselves Out Of A Man
Finally, we have the spiritually nourished woman. Whether she's new to the faith or a holy roller, her commitment to the Lord has sent men running in the opposite direction. Spiritual empowerment is often coupled with change. It's a lifestyle change that may make others feel uneasy. It usually requires a change of mind, character, behavior and relationships.

Woman who have empowered themselves spiritually may have given up a lifestyle of partying, promiscuity, drinking, alcohol, lying, cheating and a host of other worldly activities. Her spiritual integrity is often anchored by her weekly attendance at a local church. Unfortunately, it is a social atmosphere that is disproportionately female.

There is a huge gender gap within the church. For whatever reason, men just aren't into church like women are. According David Murrow, author of *Why Men Hate Going To Church*, "Every Sunday in America, more than 60 percent of the adults in our worship services are female. Almost a quarter of America's churchgoing married women worship without their husbands. Midweek gatherings often run 70 to 80 percent female. The young, single man is practically an endangered species in church today." As a result, we find an increasing number of spiritual women with no husband.

When considering these four categories, it cannot be denied that Black women are the most un-partnered group in the United States and perhaps in the world. Statistically speaking, in 2004, the Joint Center for Political and Economic Studies in Washington concluded that 42.3 percent of Black women have never been married in comparison to 16% of White women.

So, the resounding questions are "Why are so many strong and empowered Black women alone?" Is there something wrong with these women? Or is it the men? Are these women somehow broken and need to be fixed? Or do the men need to step up? Who's to blame?

In their quest to discover the reason they are alone, Black women gather at professional clubs, sorority meetings, women's groups, prayer circles and girlfriends' homes in search for an answer. They laugh, they cry, they eat good food and even talk themselves to sleep. The blame for their relational state often shifts back and forth from men to women. In all fairness, both men and women contribute to the problem. So, let's look at both sides of the equation.

Let's start with men. There are men who retreat when they come across strong and fairly successful Black women due to their own internal insecurities. In fact, there are three main factors that contribute to their adverse posture towards strong Black women. First, is the intimidation factor which plays a major role in their decision to bypass such a woman. They are intimidated by the following three things: their personality, their position, and their possessions.

Some strong Black women exhibit a very domineering, no-nonsense, opinionated and take-charge personality that may make it difficult for some men to approach. Women's status and position within society is often an area of concern for men as well. Words like doctor, lawyer, corporate executive, minister and elected official drum up concerns amongst men. Assumptions are made regarding their femininity, attitudes and their ability to co-exist with a relationship. Lastly, the obtainment of possession like a house, a car, jewelry, clothing, collectibles from around the world and the ability to afford it may play on a man's already existing insecurities.

The second factor involved in a man's abandonment of empowered Black woman is his own internal feeling of inadequacy. Rather than admiring her accomplishments, he compares himself instead. In essence, every time he looks at her it becomes a cruel reminder of what he's failed to do in his own life. As a result, he feels like he has absolutely nothing to contribute to the relationship and leaves as a consequence.

Finally, the third factor involved in a man's failure to pursue a relationship with an empowered Black woman is his traditional thinking. In a society where men are expected to be the protector and provider of the home, it's hard for many to wrap their minds around the fact that their role has been assumed by a woman. A man's inability to adapt to her ownership of this role will either cause tension or the dissolving of the relationship.

Empowered women also play a role in the failure of their relationships. First, there are women who are more successful in their careers than their partners. Such success is normally coupled with a higher earning potential which can easily shift power into a woman's lap. Unfortunately, this deviation from the traditional norm may create tension within the Black male/female relationship.

Some women carry an unhealthy attitude of superiority which exhibits itself in many ways. First, it may serve to demean and emasculate the men in their lives. Comparisons of career, personal possessions and financial contributions are made to remind him of the roles they each play in the relationship. In addition, her attempt to encourage him is often hindered due to her expression of disappointment and frustration. In many cases her verbal delivery is fueled by her feelings of resentment for shouldering most of the household's financial obligations and domestic responsibilities.

The second expression of her superiority may repel men before they would think of approaching her. One of the self-inflicted challenges women face is their need to make every personal accomplishment the new qualifier for their next relationship. In other words, whatever she's accomplished in her life often becomes a mandatory prerequisite for any man she meets.

For instance, if she has a college degree, he must also. If she makes a six figure salary, he better not be a dollar short. If she owns her own home, he can't rent. If she bench presses 210 pounds, he better come correct or not come at all.

The notion is that a man should be able to bring just as much and/or more to the table than the woman. While it is a great principle, it must be coupled with practicality. I emphatically believe that a man should be a major financial contributor in a relationship. However, some women are so rigid with their list that the only option they give themselves is to remain alone. While I agree with the concept of a list as a general guideline when meeting potential partners, it's important to be fluid and flexible when assessing potential partners.

Women also face the challenge of understanding that the skills that contribute to their success within college, the corporate workforce, the community or the church are not the skills needed to make a relationship work. In society, Black women have to be tough, self-reliant, assertive, aggressive, structured, decisive, and even opinionated at times. And it has worked successfully for them. In fact, there's much that Black men can learn from their tenacity.

The flaw comes in when empowered women decide to bring what has worked in society into their relationship. The very qualities that have caused them to succeed in the world will ultimately cause them to fail within their relationships. Why? Relationship-building requires an entirely different set of skills.

Chapter 8: _Why Black Men Don't Want You_

When a company vendor fails to deliver on a promise a swift reprimand may be appropriate; however, that approach will not work in a relationship. When negotiating with a potential client a tough and firm disposition is expected. When dealing with matters of the heart compromise is the name of the game. A fighting spirit is important on the battlefield, but a gentler spirit is needed on the home front. Unfortunately, women are winning society's battle and losing at home. The challenge is in knowing when and how to transition from work life to home life.

Lastly, some empowered women fail to prioritize a man in their lives. With so many responsibilities, obligations, and expectations placed on her, it's quite challenging to find the time and space needed to fit another person into the equation. Many women have been alone for so long that they've gotten used to functioning in a very specific way. Anything that interrupts that system can be challenging.

In pursuit of a goal, a woman may place a man so low on her list of priorities that his interest wanes. Between work, school, church, social events, and volunteering she's seldom "there" for him. She's busy being busy. Once a man discovers that very little time and space is made for him in her life, he's usually off to the next woman.

Today's women are so independent, self-sufficient and committed to their causes, that an intense focus is placed on what is before them at the expense of who is beside them.

But what does it profit a woman to gain the whole world and lose her man? Why can't she have both? Unfortunately, the misstep of not prioritizing a man in her life projects an "I don't need a man" message, though that may be far from what she desires.

In my travels, I have found that the most accomplished women desire relationships. Whether they may be college women, corporate women, church women or community women, intimacy and companionship are high up on their list of personal wants. While some are accommodating to men in their quest for love, others present a more challenging approach which sends mixed messages.

At the end of the day, Black women are disproportionately unpartnered when compared to women of other races and cultures. The blame cannot be solely placed on Black men. Both Black men and women have contributed to this harsh relational epidemic. Until we both become transparent and acknowledge what role we've played in the problem, the problem will never be solved.

Black women want to be loved, cherished and cared for. They want to be given high priority and not be chosen by process of elimination. They want to be loved for the best of who they are not rejected for the flaws and shortcomings that they exhibit in their character and behavior.

The problem with rejecting a particular group of women is that what one may be running from may be found in "the alternative" where it was not expected. White, Asian and Latin women have been bestowed a form of relational and sexual sainthood within the minds of too many men. In essence, they have been made the ideal alternative to Black women. Meanwhile, Black women have been demonized and described as self-centered, emotional tyrants who want to control the world and every man within it.

These assertions concerning the character of Black women are all sweeping generalizations that place women in a box of unfair expectations. It is almost criminal and highly insulting to unfavorably compare Black women to women of other cultures in our rationalizations for abandoning Black women. Women are all different and should not be expected to behave in the same exact ways. Their cultures are different. Their family upbringings are different. Their social standards are different.

Black women shouldn't be forced to emulate any other group. Instead, they should strive to be the best that they can be and glean from the best in all people. Meanwhile, Black men should work to develop a better sensitivity, understanding, empathy and level of commitment towards Black women in America. Both men and women doing their part will result in more partnerships, stronger families and better communities.

Chapter 9

Can A Sistah Get Some Love?

*T*here is a nation of single Black women who want and deserve to be partnered, loved, adored and valued by good Black men. But this mission appears to be an uphill battle with no foreseeable end in sight. For the last ten years I have received many phone calls, emails, and letters from distraught Black women who are frustrated with their relationships and the men in their lives. Some are so frustrated that they have even resolved to be alone for the rest of their lives.

Unfortunately, this shift in behavior is in part due to the experiences of one bad relationship after another. Right now Black women are sick and tired of being sick and tired. Many women have given up on the belief that good Black men are available. Contrary to popular belief, not all Black men are gay, gang-affiliated, on drugs, in prison, dead-beats, good-for-nothing, cheaters, only interested in White women or already married.

Even though we've socially accepted these beliefs as truth, countless Black men don't fall into these categories. Interestingly, the number one question that I receive from single Black women is "Where are these so-called good Black men at?"

The truth of the matter is that they're everywhere. You pass them on the street, in the grocery store, in the gym, at church, in school and at the library. When real men hear the statement There are no good Black men out there, they are highly offended. Sadly, the women who have bought into the 'Black male shortage' concept have either failed to see or desire the good Black men who are available.

Ironically, there are also many Black men who are beginning to say that it is hard to find a good Black woman. Obviously, there is something that is causing us to overlook each other. My objective in this chapter is to help every woman who is interested in identifying and selecting a good Black man, become able to do so.

Many women who have successfully partnered with a good Black man have unfortunately experienced lots of hardship in the process. Their journey has been met with hurt, pain, betrayal, abandonment and disappointment. As horrible as this may be, there are several contributing factors as to why this scenario continues to play out.

This entire book is laced with bold statements, examples, and stories of men's contribution to the pain women experience in their lives and relationships. This chapter will be no different. However, I do want to focus on some of the challenges that women often bring to the table that contribute to the problem as well.

Black women are regularly accused of having unrealistic expectations concerning the men that they seek. As a man, I must say that some women's expectations aren't high enough, others are very reasonable, and some are just plain ridiculous. While some are willing to settle for a man who just has all of his teeth, others are looking for men who are nothing short of perfection.

There are so many women who are in search of something they will never find: their I.B.M. (Ideal Black Man). Good Black men have often been passed up, overlooked and straight-up dissed by women who were in search of something better. As a result, Black women have become upset, frustrated and discontented by their failure to find and secure someone who only exists on television, in urban fiction, and in the imaginary minds of countless women who have been totally misled.

The Ideal Black Man is no more real than the Tooth Fairy or Santa Claus. Much like the Ideal Black Man, we've all heard the stories and seen the representation of these made-up characters but have never met them in real life. Think about it. The Tooth Fairy and Santa only show up when you are sound asleep. In essence, you have to be in a deep dreamlike state in order for them to appear. Once you awaken, they are gone. Likewise, women are simply dreaming if they think they will ever find the Ideal Black Man.

The word 'Ideal', as defined by the *American Heritage College Dictionary*, has a multitude of definitions: 1) a concept of something in its absolute perfection; 2) one seen as a standard or model of perfection or excellence. 3) existing only in the mind; imaginary; and 4) lacking practicality or the possibility of realization.

The search for someone ideal often causes women to raise the bar so high that it becomes unattainable, impractical and downright ridiculous for any man to fulfill their expectations. This, in turn, causes frustration to surface on both the part of men and women. Men often feel as if they will never measure up and leave believing that women's expectations are too high. Likewise, women's failure to secure an ideal man causes them to internalize negative feelings about themselves as well as men which often results in irrational behavior and poor decision making.

More often than not, this has caused women to go from one extreme to the next. While they were once in pursuit of an ideal that does not exist, they have later resolved that there simply aren't any good Black men at all. They have wed themselves to a belief that a good Black man is HARD to find. In reality, good Black men are everywhere. Ideal Black Men are hard to find. Nonetheless, this negative perception of Black men has deeply influenced the choices women make in dating. These women have gone from setting an unattainable bar that no man could reach, to settling for much less than they deserve.

Whether men or women are to blame for the lack of partnership, the state of relationships is getting worse each and every day. While Black men continue to indulge in a smorgasbord of dating options, countless Black women remain limited in their choices.

Alternative Dating Options Of Black Women

Women of all cultures and ethnicities often equate success with finding a man, getting married and raising a family. It is imbedded within girls at a young age. Just think about it. They are given Ken and Barbie dolls, talking babies that require changing and playhouses to keep them occupied. By the time they become of age, family is very important to them.

Generally speaking, women love the feeling of being loved and cherished. They are wired that way. So, women have a natural desire for relational intimacy. Unfortunately, in their pursuit for companionship, many wind up in less than desirable scenarios that keep them further away from acquiring that good Black man that they seek.

Several books have been written about the bad choices that good women make when choosing a partner. It has been said that they often 'look for love in all the wrong places and get into relationships for all the wrong reasons.' Whether they have been naïve, blind-sided, or simply settled for less, Black women have traveled the road most traveled by others who continue to remain unsatisfied in their relationships. The following are dating scenarios that Black women have found themselves in.

Dating Option #1: Women Who Choose Unavailable Men

The perceived shortage of African-American men has caused women to date a variety of unavailable men. However, there are three that I would like to focus on. First, some have chosen a lifestyle of man-sharing that forces women who are in a committed relationship to share their men without their knowledge. These are women who want their needs met, whether they be emotional, physical, financial, sexual or for companionship. It doesn't matter if he's married, engaged, shacking, or seriously involved.

In fact, some women intentionally seek out men who are in relationships because man-sharing has become desirable. She will justify her actions with the rationalization that the man is the other woman's responsibility, not hers. She will convince herself that she is somehow what that man needs. Endless negative outcomes result from this type of relationship. All parties are hurt in the process, including the man, his woman and the mistress.

Second, contrary to what some may believe, there are women who choose to knowingly date and marry gay and bi-sexual men. Women choose this dating option because of the perceived lack of good straight Black men. These aren't women who are oblivious to men's sexuality. Rather, they are fully aware of it and are on a mission to make them straight.

Some of these women have gay friends whom they truly love and secretly hope will one day realize that they aren't gay. It's amazing how many people are totally oblivious and irrational when it comes to homosexual desires. Black women who fall for gay men really believe that they can love the gayness right out of these men and that somehow, their stuff is so good that it can magically cure any man's same-sex desires. These women believe that by providing a warm home and loving family, their gay love interest will never desire to look at another man again. Well, I can assure you that the cure-all is not found in a woman's lips, hips or fingertips.

Third, there are women who choose to stand behind their men, while their men are forced to stand behind bars. For some women all bets are off once their man winds up in jail. However, there are a growing number of women who choose to stick around regardless of the prison term. Whether they're sentenced to 20 days or 20 years, some women have committed to be ride-or-die chicks for life. If this reality is too hard for you to grasp just turn on your radio and you will hear a litany of 'lock-down love dedications' given from women to their inmate lovers.

While it may seem admirable for women to hold it down till their beau gets out of lock-down, it's potentially risky as well. Whether the inmate is guilty or innocent of the crime committed is not the only issue. The major problem is the prison culture that comes along with dating an inmate. There's a whole lot of mess that goes on 'Behind Da Wall.'

In many cases, it's an environment defined by physical violence, sexual violence, situational sexuality, lies, tricks and deception. Prisoners exist in an environment where gangs, drugs, AIDS, rape and assault, prisoner-on-prisoner sex, prisoner-on-staff sex and all other types of deplorable acts run rampant.

Too many sisters hang in there hoping and praying for a change to come, thinking that the letters, erotic pictures, and sexy outfits on visitation day will help to secure their man. Instead, it keeps them in an indefinite holding pattern which often ends in frustration. While every inmate's relationship should be evaluated and judged on a case-by-case basis, it is often a parasitic relationship with no substantial benefit to the women involved.

Dating Option #2: Women Who Date Outside of Their Race

Traditionally, Black women have been loyal to Black men. Regardless of how good or bad the relationship, their allegiance has been commendable. However, in recent times, more women are beginning to see dating outside the race as a viable option. As more Black women become serious about marriage and commitment, a lot are starting to believe that the pickings are slim. So, they're choosing to date brown, red, yellow and white.

There are a number of reasons why Black women choose to date outside of their race. First, the numbers don't work in their favor. There are considerably more available Black women than available Black men. The unavailability of Black men may be due to incarceration, low educational and economic status and possible substance abuse.

Second, the daily social settings of successful Black women typically are void of any significant number of Black men. As a result, they work and socialize with men from other ethnicities which may possibly lead to dating relationships. Third, Black women are simply not waiting for the Ideal Black Man and have opened up their options to find love and happiness.

There are a number of personal reasons why Black women choose to date outside of their race. I asked a number of Black women why they date White men, and their reasons include the following:

- They are more emotionally available
- They are open to long-term relationships
- They don't play childish games
- They don't attempt to dominate every aspect of the relationship
- They respect you
- They really know how to treat Black women
- They are romantic
- They don't abuse you
- They have fewer hang-ups about oral sex and foreplay
- They communicate and tell you what's on their minds
- They compliment you and make you feel appreciated
- They had fathers at home who were role models
- The physical differences between the races are exciting

As wonderful as this list depicts White men, upon closer inspection, not all interracial relationships are what they are cracked up to be. In fact, many are just like any other relationship. Some are good. Some are bad. Women who choose to date outside their race must make sure their expectations are couched in reality and not cultural stereotypes that paint a one-dimensional view of any group of people.

Dating Option # 3: Women Who Date Like Men

The woman who dates like a man has made the decision to take on the posture of a man regarding sex, dating and relationships. Her mentality is clear, "Because men have sexed women for so long and gotten away with it, it's my turn to return the favor." So, she will become just as ruthless as a man to prove that she can win at the sex game. The problem is, many innocent bystanders are hurt and made victims in the process just as women have been for so many years.

Though it may shock you, but many women desire sex just as much as men do. They think about it, fantasize about it, crave it and will go to clubs, bars and social events to get it. Their number one priority is their own physical gratification. They will often date several men simultaneously. They're not really looking for a commitment. Their mentality is "I'll do my thing and you do your thing."

In many cases, she refuses to tie herself down in a relationship. Therefore, she chooses only to date, thus allowing her to be free from a lifestyle of monogamy. She can do whoever and however many she chooses.

While writing this book, I came across a woman who we will call Tamika. She's a 37 year-old and twice-divorced-woman who has chosen to date like a man. After being in one bad relationship after another she admitted:

"I have had 29 sexual encounters in the course of one year. There were no strings attached. No feelings hurt. Even though I was never satisfied, I continued to have sex with men in order to seek vengeance on all the men who hurt me in my past. There was no touching, hugging or kissing. It was just straight sex. Once it was over, I would tell them all to leave."

While this dating option may appear to be a form of women's liberation, it actually keeps them bound in a state of unhealthy relationships (sexships) which produce no meaningful, long-lasting results. Though, their ultimate goal is to obtain a healthy relationship, their actions work against that effort.

Dating Option # 4: Friends With Benefits

As hard as it may sound, men generally control the dating scene. Whatever they want, they typically get because women know that the gender numbers don't work in their favor. A woman may believe that in order to get and keep a man, she has to play by his rules. While most women want commitment, most men want sex. The mentality for many women is, 'In order to get what I want, I have to play by his rules.

So, men will draw women into a sex-ship instead of a well-balanced, committed relationship. Women then offer sex in hopes of eventually winning a man over into a relationship. However, it is often not until their hearts are broken that these women learn that giving sex may motivate him to do many things, but commitment is usually not one of them. Why? Their belief is consistent with the old expression 'why buy the cow if you can get the milk for free?'

This poor state of affairs has caused women to give up on relationships. In fact, women who can't establish committed relationships may settle for the next best thing: friends with benefits. The fact is, very few friends with benefits (sex-ships) ever turn into real, long-term, committed relationships. These unhealthy connections come and go, but there are women who hold onto them for a sense of fulfillment and companionship that does not last.

Much like the woman who dates like a man, this woman is tired of being hurt and disappointed in relationships. So, rather than deal with another strained relationship, she may opt to have sexual dealings with no strings attached. Rather than constantly become vulnerable, many choose to sex men until they find their soul mate. This way, in their minds, nobody gets hurt. So, she settles for a lifestyle of late-night and/or early-morning calls which lead to nothing beyond a lustful exchange between two consenting individuals.

Though no emotions are required to partake in such an activity, there is usually a connection between the caller and the callee. The connection represents a certain level of trust and familiarity that the two parties have with one another. Though each person is free to sex whomever they choose, the connection between the two helps them justify their activity as being more than meaningless casual sex.

Most women trapped in this dating situation aren't typically happy or fulfilled. In fact, this arrangement may create frustration and insecurities in the woman. After weeks, months and even years of uncommitted sexual relations, she feels she's earned a certain level of commitment from him that he's not willing to give. Ultimately, these agreed upon relationships wane with women feeling more distraught than they were when it all first began.

Dating Option #5: Women Who Choose Other Women

The relational tides are turning for many women. With one bad relationship after another, Black women are deciding to seek intimate partnerships with other women. A clear change is taking place with sexual orientation and more people than ever before are making the decision to change allegiances.

Women are deciding to step out of their conventional gender box for a variety of reasons. Some women are simply tired of the game playing, the insensitivity, the limited dating pool of men, and the downright disrespect they've endured in their relationships. Fed up with men altogether, they are deciding to make the gender switch. They've convinced themselves that only a woman knows what another woman truly needs and wants. So they seek out their gender counterparts to meet their emotional, mental, and sexual needs.

However, during their exploration, many come to find out that same-sex relationships "ain't no crystal stair." In fact, some can be just as unhealthy as heterosexual relationships. Therefore, the gender switch isn't the real answer to their problems. In Sister Souljah's book, *No Disrespect*, she writes:

"Women, too can be power hungry exploiters. Women can also be two-time, low down cheats. Women can also be emotionally abusive and insensitive. Do not believe that same sex love will solve your problems. You can be hurt in any human relationship. Leaving your man because you have experienced pain, only to sleep with another woman will not guarantee that you will be treated more kindly, with greater tenderness, and with more respect. Women are abusers just like men. Confront your inner confusion before you enter into any relationship."

While some choose women out of relational frustration, others choose women to keep from cheating on their man with other men. These are women who may be physically separate from their partners but maintain commitment in a very unique way. These women may be married to or dating men in prison or in the military serving overseas.

In their attempt to remain loyal, they develop emotional and sexual attachments with women in order to prevent the possibility of sexual indiscretions with other men. Both the woman and the male have somehow convinced themselves that a sexual relationship with another woman doesn't constitute as cheating. So, a woman will fulfill her sexual needs by replacing a man's penis with a strap-on, dildo, or vibrator. Somehow, the shaft of a real penis inserted into a woman's vagina is an abomination. But a woman bringing another woman to climax is an acceptable practice. Whether male or female, once intimacy takes place, emotional attachment soon follows. So, a love affair with a woman can be just as crushing as one with a man.

Whether due to past pain, current unavailability or circumstantial conditions more and more women are choosing to kindle a romantic flame with their own kind. Unfortunately, this trend will continue to develop if Black male/female interpersonal relationships don't get any better.

Dating Option #6: Women Who Date Down

Whether good or bad, women often raise their standards for men as they become more accomplished. For instance, if a woman obtains a college degree she will more than likely seek a man who has obtained the same. If she earns an impressive salary, she expects his salary to at least be comparable. If she has a personal relationship with God, he is expected to at least be committed to a church. In all fairness, these are reasonable requests. Every woman should want a man to be an equal contributor in the relationship.

The challenge that Black women face may not be compared to the challenges faced by women of other ethnic groups. African Americans are the only race of people where the women

177

outperform their men in the areas of education and employment. It then becomes challenging for some who are moderately successful to find a companion who is comparable in the same areas. If and when these women choose to commit to a man who doesn't measure up (financially and educationally), they consider themselves to be 'dating down'.

The phraseology 'Dating Down' typically strikes a nerve with men. To imply that a woman is dating down because of a man's financial/educational status places a very narrow view on his manhood. The terminology also implies a disposition of superiority on the woman's part. The phrase positions her on a higher plane which requires her to step down to his level. This concept creates a competitive atmosphere within the relationship which detracts from the oneness that should be developed within it.

Black women shouldn't be forced to make the choice between love and financial security within a relationship. It should be a package deal. However, for too many women, a variety of factors keep this from being a reality. Therefore, there are women who want companionship who forego certain relational pre-requisites and choose the option to 'Date Down'.

Dating Option #7: Women Who Dumb It Down

One of the major drawbacks of a woman's success is her inability to share it with the one she's with. There are men who are repelled by women who are more knowledgeable, more experienced and more accomplished than them. This may be the result of insecurities, inadequacies, or traditional thinking which keeps women limited to certain roles.

Therefore, some Black women feel as if they have to conceal their true identity and accomplishments in order to accommodate a man. Some have downplayed their degrees, job titles and positions, financial status, and the neighborhoods they live in for fear that they may be pre-judged and disqualified. Some have even downplayed their intellect and choice of vocabulary to keep a man from feeling intimidated. Beyond dollars and degrees, women often give up their interests and passions in exchange for companionship as well.

This all too familiar scenario is creating a major sense of frustration in Black women. It's unfair that they have to be forced to 'dumb it down' just to get and keep a man. Sadly, some men think that if a woman articulates or celebrates her accomplishments in front of a man, she's somehow emasculating him. One woman said it best: "It's almost as if your paycheck alone could paper-cut their balls right off." As humorous as the statement may sound, it speaks to the dire state of African-American relationships.

This dating option produces a lose-lose for both parties involved. The woman loses because she's forced to deny the power of her existence. The man loses because a) the concealment of her true essence keeps him from being challenged to be and do more, and b) a later discovery of her multi-faceted identity may create resentment, trust issues and may possibly dissolve the relationship. In the end, honesty is the best policy. If you have to 'dumb it down' to validate someone else's ego, it's a relationship not worth having.

In most cases, the previously mentioned dating options are scenarios women have settled for because of their possible inability to secure a good Black man. But what about when a woman comes across a good Black man and he's still not enough?

You're A Great Guy But...

One of the most contentious discussions between Black men and women is the notion of what Black women really want in a man. Frankly, men are confused. They often express to me that there is a conflict between what women say they want in a man versus what they are attracted to. Many women declare that they want a good, God-fearing, professional, hard-working, vision-having, sensitive, faithful, committed and husband-like man. However, many self-proclaimed 'good Black men' or 'nice guys' complain that they are often overlooked.

179

It has been said that 'nice guys always come in last place'. Well, these men fit the bill. They are often told that they are 'too nice' or 'too corny'. They are passed up for not being down or hood enough. That somehow they lack swagger. One educated Black male said that men in his circle get passed up for guys of a "thuggier" nature. Many of educated/professional women want the 'Tupac with a degree' type of brother. You know, the brother with swag who's known for being a lady's man.

Meanwhile, nice guys often hear how wonderful they are and how they will make some woman happy one day. These are the guys who come with a steady flow of compliments, flowers and candy, open doors, pull out chairs, a coat to keep you warm and thoughtful gifts. They are thoughtful, gentle, respectful, emotionally transparent, good conversationalists, and are concerned with what they can do for you rather than what they can get from you. But there is seldom any apparent reward for their behavior.

They are told 'don't change a thing'...'hang in there'...'you'll find her someday'...'just be yourself'...'you're a great guy but...'. They typically get put in the 'Just Friends', 'B.F.F. '(best friends forever), or 'Cuddle Buddy' category. They become the person who provides the safe, friendly environment with no reasonable expectation of complications, drama or progression of the friendship to "something more". Ironically, they are what women often say they wanted in a man but often ignore.

Not all nice guys are alone waiting to be noticed. Many have secured women in dating, committed relationships and even marriage. And for many, their relationships have worked successfully. However, I've heard about so many brothers who cook, clean, help with the kids, work hard all day, don't cheat on their women and attempt to please them in every way possible. Ironically, these are the ones who are left by their women for being 'too good', 'too nice' or just plain 'BORING'.

I recently watched an episode of *Divorce Court*, which can be seen on the video clips page of my website http://www.whywehateblackwomen.com. It featured a woman who was divorcing her husband for being too nice. In her own words she explained her problem with the relationship: "We were like best friends. I believe he was my soul mate. Everything was fine except he was too nice. It was like scary nice. It's too good to be true. He would say 'I love you' and I was waiting for the punch. When are you gonna kick me? It's scary! He's a wonderful man. I'm just not used to that."

Whether you consider reality courtroom television a credible source of information or not, this particular relationship dynamic truly does exist. Unfortunately, there are quite a few women who suffer from all types of anxieties, self esteem issues and feelings of unworthiness. Therefore, they don't always feel like they are deserving of someone who will treat them right. Others who have experienced one bad relationship after the next may feel uncomfortable or suspicious of good treatment. While conducting several interviews with women regarding this issue, I've received some very honest responses.

We dream about the perfect man but many times when he comes along our own insecurities creep in about being with Mr. Perfect and deep down we don't feel like we are worthy of having him. Why...because of past relationships and experiences, we fear that he will start off a saint and end up like Lucifer.

Ericka, 36, Fitness Instructor

I have a sister who prefers the thug type; when she tried to step outside of that box and deal with a guy who worked, wanted to take her out and treat her like a woman she said she 'wasn't used to that' and it was 'weird' to her. She eventually went back to her abusive, good-for-nothing boyfriend.

Kendra, 23, Student

Why We Hate Black Women

Ladies lie but looks and swag count – so even though he may not be stable or as courteous many of us will give that up for the bad boy aura. Sometimes women can be our own worst enemy.

Su, 32, Adminstrator

The response of the 'nice guy' to this unfortunate dating dilemma can never be predicted. Their reactions vary greatly. Some continue to wait on the sidelines as they observe less deserving men secure many of these women. Some try their luck with women of other nationalities who may be more accepting of their overall style and personality. Some totally flip the script and become playas in order to gain popularity amongst the ladies.

However, once they get one, these women's efforts are spent trying to turn them into the men they've always avoided. Others remain exactly how they are and patiently wait for the right one to come along. Interestingly, most women grow out of the 'bad boy' stage at some point in their lives and want to settle down with the 'nice guy' they've spent their lives avoiding. Case in point, one woman told me:

"I have a friend who was the 'not as cool' friend, now he is a shameless player. He is still short, wears glasses, dresses preppy, loves golf, has a well respected job, is a conversationalist and helps everyone. But all types of women are clamoring over him. He is now the man we want to marry. Now he has a girlfriend and a back-up. In fact, he has several back-ups. Women are fighting over the former nerd and he is playing us lovely. See nice guys are only in fashion when marriage is required.

Janet, 30, Social Worker

So 'nice guys' and 'good Black men' do appear to get the women they want in the end. Unfortunately, many are often stuck waiting around to enjoy the companionship they seek. But for now, Black women continue to choose men who aren't necessarily good for them. In some respects, it appears that the thug (playa, bad boy, etc.) has become the man of choice among women of diverse age, educational and occupational categories.

Generally speaking, young ladies between their early teen years to their mid-thirties have a fascination for bad boys. Some women don't outgrow this type of man at all. These are men who are known for living on the edge. They take pleasure in pushing the envelope and deviating from socially acceptable behaviors. They often go after what they want with a focus and determination that women find extremely exciting. They are usually men with a backbone, beliefs they stand by and possess a hyper-masculine energy that women often find irresistible.

As one woman put it: *"I don't like the thug per say, but I want a man, a real man who can defend himself when it matters, and who can have my back emotionally and physically."* Women want to feel protected and secure and the bad boy is believed to provide that reality. Lastly, bad boys are thought to exude a type of confidence not found in the typical 'nice guy.'

When a woman says a man is too nice, she typically means that a guy lacks charisma, charm and the confidence that it takes to make a woman feel passionate and interested. She sees him as a wimp, milquetoast, too sensitive and soft like a woman. While the bad boy will stand up for himself, the 'nice guy' will typically put up with her behavior no matter how negative it may be. He's more easygoing, non-confrontational, and willing to go along with her plan as long as it's pleasing to her. In the end, she looks at him as being a doormat that can be easily controlled and manipulated. Once this happens, all respect is lost.

I know a few women who say they want a good man/spouse, but when they get him, they disrespect and mistreat him, leaving him high and dry for the no-good bama they "claim" they don't want. Then sistahs like me have to go through the fire and flood to come across one of these good brothas...by the time they've been used and abused and make it to us, they're skeptical and hesitant about being in a great, long-term relationship. It's a vicious cycle that must end.

Nyisha, 26, Educator

A lot of women were not taught to appreciate the gifts that lies within a man. We as women (not all but majority) have been taught the 'get yours girl while the getting is good mentality' or the 'use what you got to get what you want out of a man' mentality!!! Which is messed up anyway you look at it, but it is reality.

Debra, 35, Transit Worker

Meanwhile, women who are drawn to certain qualities within the 'bad boy' or 'thug' are forced to deal with a whole bag of issues. In all fairness, there are men who are 'rough around the edges' who know how to treat a woman with the utmost respect. Their street life doesn't necessarily disqualify them from having a wonderful relationship with a woman.

However, there are others who give all Black men a bad name. Certainly not in all cases, but often enough women become constantly disappointed, physically and verbally abused, continuously cheated on and financially taken advantage of. Just read some of the responses of the women I interviewed.

I had a thug. He talked down to me, he choked me, and at one point he put a gun to my face when we fought. I stayed with him for a year and went as far as planning a wedding with him...Go figure. As women we sometimes look for that father figure or that bad guy to make us feel secure and the ones we can run all over we don't give them the time of day.

Daramis, 35, Health Specialist

I currently work at a fairly large company and there are many women here who are barely making it because they have a thug at home who does not work or do anything for them. Whenever I ask why they stay I always get the same answer. They love him and eventually he will get himself together. I have seen women lose good positions because of drug charges that were not their fault but because the house was in their name it was their problem. These women spend countless amounts of money on bail, child support and lawyers to name a few. The sad part is that if they were to leave them, they would wind up with another thug. They like the look, the feel and lifestyle that the thug brings. Basically they are addicted to Drama.

Jasmine, 37, Insurance Adjustor

As sad as it is, there are women who are easily bored and are drawn to drama. So, a man with a steady job, his own place, a good future, and a college education is not enough. Some of the women that I've interviewed have admitted that they no longer care about a man with a good job, an education, goals or a desire to commit. They have enough means to take care of themselves. As long as he can 'put it down' (sex) and create a level of excitement he qualifies.

After speaking with people across the country on relationships for the past twelve years I've discovered that we all have different tastes and tolerances in the men and women we choose. So, when all is said and done, it would be almost pointless for me to tell anyone who they should or should not be attracted to. However, what I can do is provide you with certain guidelines that may help guide your attraction in a more personally beneficial direction.

Go On Girl, Get Your Man

First, the key to finding the right guy is to know exactly what it is that you're looking for. Some women wind up with men who don't fit the bill because they haven't clearly established what it is they really want. People often know what they don't want but are uncertain about what they do want.

Secondly, women may have a list of qualities that men must possess. And just about every now and then a brother comes along who represents everything on the list. However, he may arrive in a package that she does not approve of. He may be mentally and spiritually appealing but lacks the physical appearance that she requires in a man. For instance, he may not be tall enough, thin enough, or dark enough. He may not dress with enough swag or be cool enough.

Sometimes we allow the most trivial things to keep us from finding true happiness. One woman actually admitted, "the fact that he bites his fingernails is creepy to me." I mean, come on! Like so many others, she wants the picture perfect man: someone who is flawless. More than a lack of available good Black men, her unwillingness to compromise is what has kept her alone. Meanwhile, some of these same women complain about the no good men they're dating and the drama that goes along with it.

Women who date well and ultimately marry understand the fine art of compromise. They also demand from themselves the same thing they demand and expect from a potential partner.

They realize that Mr. Right isn't going to be Mr. Perfect. In fact, even the most desirable men in the world have serious issues, flaws and weakness that must be addressed.

One of men's biggest requests for women is to be more open-minded about the possibilities of dating. Stop getting caught up in trivial things that have nothing to do with ultimate happiness. If certain attributes really don't make that much of a difference in the larger scheme of things, accept them rather than rule out a potentially meaningful relationship because of things that just don't matter. In essence, focus on the worth of a person's substance above style.

Don't get me wrong. I'm not suggesting that you tolerate someone or something that goes against your core values in life. However, it's important to understand that lots of men are diamonds in the rough and certain things can simply be worked on. Extra pounds can be shed, crooked teeth can be fixed and clothing fashions can be updated. The list just goes on and on.

In order to secure a good Black man, it's important to know what a good Black man is. If you were to ask ten different women to provide a definition you would most likely receive ten different responses. Why? It's simple. The answer is based upon a woman's age, maturity level, experience, interests, passions, personal needs, desires and expectations.

What may be good to a college-aged woman may be different than what's good to a forty-five year old woman who is a single parent. So, in your quest to find a good man, it's important to properly assess yourself first and then make wise choices based upon that assessment. So, for a thorough analysis that will help you find a good man go to www.whywehateblackwomen.com and take Hasani's Relationship Questionnaire. It is a comprehensive questionnaire that will help you clarify what you're looking for in a potential date/mate.

After completing the questionnaire you will soon discover that a good man is not going to meet every item on your checklist, nor should he. If he did, that would make him ideal (perfect). He is human with frailties and faults mixed in with all of his wonderful qualities. When dating, you have to apply the 80/20 rule. If a man has 80% of what you are looking for, you've found a pretty good catch. The other 20% can either be tolerated or worked on.

The problem is that many of us, both male and female, will complain about a person's failure to obtain the remaining twenty percent. We will give up the eighty in search for the remaining twenty and wind up worse off than we were when we started.

In any event, if you follow my system you will avoid the unfavorable dating options outlined earlier in the chapter. It will serve to put you on the path to true love. Keep in mind, this one step is only the beginning of the process to secure a great relationship. But, it is a good start.

Chapter 10

Black Women Are Hated...Now What?

*"Focus 90% of your time on solutions and only 10% of your time
on problems."*
~Anthony J. D'Angelo

ongratulations, you have successfully reached the final chapter of this book. I hope that the pages of this manuscript answered certain questions and raised several others. By now I'm sure some of you are pondering the question "Now what?"

Many of us have grandiose ideas of what we would like to see and experience in the Black community. However, none of it can be achieved if our personal lives aren't in order. We need to take the time to self-reflect and begin to work on our issues. We must remember that we are the lowest common denominator in each and every relationship that we enter into. How? It's simple. We take us everywhere we go. So, if we jump from one bad relationship to the next, sometimes we have to take a good look at ourselves first.

This chapter is dedicated to resolving many of the challenges presented in this book. They are not cure-alls. They are simply suggestions to help place you on the path of change and transformation. My hope is that you spend a considerable amount of your time in this chapter. Use it as a guide to help you plot your personal and relational course in life. Sometimes all it takes is one or two adjustments to create new positive effects in your life. As you read, keep in mind that each section will recap a previous chapter and offer a tangible solution to be considered.

Black Women Are Valued By No One...

"Black women are valued by no one..." is a very provocative statement. The three dots that follow the statement are called an ellipsis. It is typically used to represent an intentional silence. It implies that a further thought was intended but not expressed. So, let me bring additional clarity to the statement.

Black women have been so mishandled in this society that it seems as though they are valued by no one. Certainly, there is a community of Black people who care for and love Black women. However, as a group, Black women have suffered at the hands of others due to their race and gender. They truly are a double minority. But don't let that limit you. Don't let it plot the course of your life. Don't allow others to take advantage of your race and sexuality.

If you've been in a physically abusive relationship learn how to break the cycle. If you're currently in one, get far away from that person. Leave the state if you have to. There are places that an abused woman can go to get help. Don't stay thinking he will change. It can only get worse. Get help right away. Don't blame yourself. Don't try to protect and help change the behavior of the abuser. Don't keep it a secret and internalize the pain. Just get out and seek help.

If you have been sexually abused get help. Stop protecting your abuser. Stop blaming yourself. Stop allowing family and friends to manipulate you out of telling your story, pressing charges, seeking help and freeing yourself of self-blame. Don't be intimidated by public opinion that says 'it was your fault' or 'you should have known better.' Stop carrying the pain, guilt, and bitterness bottled up inside of you.

If you've been unfairly treated or discriminated against because of your race, stand up and fight for your rights. Don't be intimidated by employers, police officers and all other powers that be when you fall prey to injustice. Remember, God and the law is on your side.

In a society where Black women are not valued in the media, in music, in corporate America, in our churches and in many of our families and relationships, it's time to find a place of solace. First, learn to value yourself. Then seek out those who truly value you and allow them to build a fortress of love, respect and admiration around you.

Create a community of people who will celebrate your uniqueness, not tear you down. Seek out healthy people and pursue healthy relationships. When a person truly has a community of support, they have all the ammunition they need to face the world.

Too Strong For Your Own Good

Contrary to popular belief, being strong, Black, independent and female can be hazardous to your health. In fact, it can be deadly. This chapter began with a quote from an unknown female poet who wrote, "Being a strong black woman is killing us softly." Though difficult to accept, this chapter was written for the purpose of building a strong case in support of that statement.

This chapter is a plea for women to redefine their strength in a way that benefits them. This message is part of the same story that Sojourner Truth, Zora Neale Hurston, Bell Hooks, Toni Morrison and others have told for years. It's time to redefine Black womanhood.

How many mothers, grandmothers, and sister-friends do you know who reflect the Strong Black Woman described within this text? How many women do you know who have suffered in silence, denied their hopes and become hardened by choices that have contributed to their internal demise?

For all women who have a need to constantly give of themselves, consider the words of health and fitness consultant Erica Lewis.

"Strong means wisdom; being able to make proper and effective decisions at the right time that will be long lasting, conducive and advantageous for everyone involved – your husband, your kids, your community, your teammates and yourself. Women often think that strength means doing everything. Sometimes with wisdom, the strength of saying no is more powerful than the strength of saying yes."

If you're in a relationship, your strength should be an asset not a liability. Make sure it remains a gift to be cherished, not a curse to be feared. Use your strength to compliment your partner not to compete with him. He doesn't need to hear how much you don't need him and how well you can do on your own. Instead, he needs to know that you are capable of being self-sufficient if need be, but that you value the support that he brings to the table. So let him fully operate in his role.

Let a man be a man. By that, I mean if you are dating or are committed to a man who is responsible, handles his business and knows how to lead, let him. Some women have been in charge of everything for so long that it is often a challenge to trust and hand over that responsibility to someone else.

Let him treat you like a lady. It has been said that chivalry is dead and women have killed it. Some women have erroneously taught 'Don't let a man do nothing for you. Do everything for yourself.' This is ridiculous. If that man wants to open your car door, let him. If he wants to pull out your chair, let him. If he wants to help you with your coat, let him. If he wants to buy you a gift, let him. If he wants to pay for the meal, let him. Let him be the man and take care of you.

The following parable speaks directly to those who exhibit an unhealthy form of strength and independence in their lives.

'There was a man all alone; he had neither son nor brother. There was no end to his toil, yet his eyes were not content with his wealth. "For whom am I toiling," he asked, "and why am I depriving myself of enjoyment?" This too is meaningless— a miserable business! Two are better than one, because they have a good return for their work: If one

falls down, his friend can help him up. But pity the man who falls and
has no one to help him up!
Ecclesiastes 4:8-10

The parable has one very clear message. There is strength and
unity in numbers. Much like the 'Strong Black Woman', the man
in the parable worked independently. However, he quickly came to
realize the benefits of receiving assistance from others. That, in
fact, two are better than one. What he initially described as
meaningless and miserable work soon rendered him a sizeable
return once he was willing to receive help from others. What a
powerful lesson.

In conclusion, it's time to redefine and embrace the true
meaning of strength and do away with the Strong Black Woman
and Superwoman stereotype which has no apparent reward.
Instead, hold onto your God-given strength and learn how to
properly navigate with it in society, in relationship with others and
most importantly within yourself.

The Tale About Black Tail

More than two hundred years after the life and death of Sarah
Baartman, we continue to place the Black behind on a pedestal.
Women of all nationalities have gone to great lengths to obtain
and/or display what Saartjie "Sarah" Baartman spent the later
portion of her life trying to escape: being labeled "just another
piece of Black tail". But your worth extends well beyond the size
and shape of your backside.

In 2005, India Arie wrote a song for Black women entitled *I
Am Not My Hair*. The song quickly became an empowering
anthem for sistahs who have always struggled with their identity,
with European standards of beauty, or simply with what to do with
their hair. Arie's transformative lyrics are as follows:

Why We Hate Black Women

I looked in the mirror
For the first time and saw that HEY....
I am not my hair
I am not this skin
I am not your expectations no no
I am not my hair
I am not this skin
I am a soul that lives within

(Whoa, whoa, whoa)
Does the way I wear my hair make me a better person?
(Whoa, whoa, whoa)
Does the way I wear my hair make me a better friend? Oooh
(Whoa, whoa, whoa)
Does the way I wear my hair determine my integrity?
(Whoa, whoa, whoa)
I am expressing my creativity...
(Whoa, whoa, whoa)

What a powerful message. So many women were liberated by this song. India's song set so many women free from the shackles of people's expectations of their hair. Well, if it can work for hair, it can work for any other body part. Simply exchange the word hair with backside. Now ask yourself a simple list of questions: Does my backside make me a better person? Does my backside make me a better friend? Does my backside determine my integrity? The answer is emphatically NO!

Sarah Baartman was made to feel ugly because she had a big butt. Now women are made to feel ugly if they don't sport a big butt. Something is seriously wrong with society when we determine a person's worth based upon physical dimensions. Regardless of physical stature, Black women need to continue to love themselves from the outside in, as well as, the inside out.

Discover the beauty that lies within you. Stop trying to measure up to society's standard of beauty. Take the time to understand that you were fearfully and wonderfully made no matter how big or small your butt may be. Psalms 139:14 reads, "I will praise you, for I am fearfully and wonderfully made; marvelous are your works, and my soul knows very well."

The next time you have the temptation to question your body image just remember that you were created in God's perfect image. If God's image of you is perfect, that means He made no mistakes in your physical stature. He designed you to be exactly who He wanted you to be inside and out. So when you apply physical scrutiny to denigrate yourself, it is a direct slap in God's face. There is no room in your life for low self-image and self perception. Take the time to realize your truth worth.

What makes a woman golden is not her thighs, her breasts, her hips, or her backside. The foundation of her womanhood can be found in her virtue. So look in the mirror and tell yourself, "I am fearfully and wonderfully made! I am fearfully and wonderfully made! I-am-fearfully-and wonderfully-made!!!!!"

Hatred In The Name of Hip Hop

Rap music is certainly not responsible for starting the abuse, assault or rape of Black women, but some of it does advocate, glorify, justify and condone it. This type of rap music works to reinforce and ensure the continuation and survival of these evils. Anyone who participates in the rap industry must acknowledge their responsibility for the impact of the images and messages on the minds of impressionable youth.

It's easy to point the finger at the rappers exclusively and denounce their attitudes and lyrics. But essentially, everyone who, in one fashion or another, supports this form of Hip-Hop is to blame. Each Black woman who makes a conscious choice to be out on the floor dancing and singing to this entertainment must realize that they are the ones who are being degraded by these lyrics.

The rapper belting forth his latest hit is not going to mention you by name, but the message he's sending out is that all Black women are the same, and should be treated the same. They may very well say they are only referring to the gold-digging groupies and strippers out there. However, their depiction of women is often one-dimensional and leaves its audience with no other option but to view all Black women in that one way.

So, if you, as a Black woman, think that the labels, "b-tch" and "ho" are only relegated to the women in the videos, you're naïve and sadly mistaken. These derogatory terms are aimed at you, whether or not you want to acknowledge it.

The sad fact is that everyone out there is responsible in some way. In the words of Edmund Burke, "All it takes for evil to succeed is for good men to stand and do nothing." Every time we purchase a Hip-Hop CD or watch a video that portrays Black women in a negative fashion, *we* are to blame. We are creating a demand for more of the same, and are essentially telling the recording industry and rappers that "it's just fine – treat us however you want – we'll keep supporting you."

Ultimately, what you're seeing is an inter-racial alliance between Black and White men who are reaping tremendous profits from the overt exploitation of this over-sexualized Black female image. Asian execs, producers, writers, and artists are also attempting to cash in on the subjugated Black female sexuality. As a result, Hip Hop enterprising has created an assembly line production (CDs, DVDs and magazines) which amount to a gang rape of Black female identity.

In fact, the trend amongst corporate execs can easily be summed up in the depiction of the now infamous image of a man swiping a credit card through the crack of a Black female's backside in rap star Nelly's video *Tip Drill*. That five second video bite exposes the way many rappers, the recording industry and their eager clientele view Black women: as a commodity or a piece of property. Their value is only determined by the degree to which they can be violated.

It is also important to note that while Nelly caught the heat for the credit swipe incident it was the video model's idea. Women are equal and willing participants in their own degradation. Their love for attention, money and status has caused them to fully embrace their sexually exploitive role. In order for Hip Hop to change its direction, Black female strippers, groupies, models, rappers, and those behind the camera must decide that enough is enough.

The female participants, the recording moguls, the rappers, the DJs, the radio station programmers, the music corporate execs, the listeners, and the consumers all have a share in the perpetuation of Black female debasement. You, the listener, is just as responsible as the rapper that penned the lyrics, or the choreographer who laid out the video. Everyone who accepts and supports this demoralization is to blame. But the tides are beginning to turn.

The Hip Hop messages of violence, misogyny, female hyper-sexuality, and degradation are beginning to reach a boiling point with many Black women. While some continue to shake their tail feather on the dance floor and drop it like its hot every time they hear misogynist lyrics placed over a tight beat, others stand in protest. Fortunately, Black women are beginning to realize that their image has suffered immeasurably, and that it is time to take a stand and refuse to be treated so degradingly.

While it is good that some Black women are finally taking a stand against the oppressive forces within the music industry, they should not be alone. For centuries Black women have had to fend for themselves while many Black men have sat on the sidelines and watched the cultural/gender assault unfold. It is now time for Black men to redeem the time that has been lost, fight for and stand with Black women.

Hip Hop is a wonderful art-form of cultural expression. However, it should not be used as a tool in the gender war against Black women. Rather, it must be a vehicle for cultural pride. Therefore, Black men and Black women must join forces and collectively work towards a proper and balanced portrayal of Black women within Hip hop music and culture.

Black, Female & Mad As Hell

For years Black women have generally been stereotyped as bearing an attitude of anger, hostility and bitterness. Rightly or wrongly, they've been perceived as overly sensitive, emotional, and verbally insulting. However, women of other ethnicities who display the same outward expressions or behaviors are not stigmatized in the same way. They are seen as someone who is apparently having a bad day.

Black women, on the other hand, aren't given a pass. Just think about it. If you suck your teeth, you're angry. If you roll your eyes, you're angry. If you talk too loud, you're angry. If you breathe too hard, you're angry. If you sigh in disappointment, you're angry. If you make the wrong facial expression, you're angry. No matter what you do, corporate America, the media, society and unfortunately many of our own people will peg you as an 'Angry Black Woman'.

There's a great lesson to be learned here. All Black women are "guilty" of being angry, whether they are angry in reality or "angry" according to someone else's perception. Undeniably, some women are angry bitter souls, but others have been misunderstood and falsely perceived. So, which one are you? Only you and those who really know you can truly answer that question.

While some of you can honestly admit and acknowledge your struggle, others either aren't aware or deny all forms of its existence. Wherever you may find yourself, certain steps can be taken to move from bitter to better.

As mentioned in earlier chapters, several factors have contributed to the disposition that so many of our women possess. There may be things your family, friends or love interests have done in your past, even decades ago that have caused you pain. Rather than moving forward, you continue to dwell on past issues and problems that keep you trapped in your past. You may even find yourself reliving certain conversations or experiences that were unpleasant or traumatizing, thus causing you to become angry again and again and again.

When you carry an attitude with you wherever you go, the world is negatively affected by it. The Bible even says in Proverbs 25:24, "Better to live on a corner of a roof than to share a home with a quarreling (angry) woman." But not only does your anger seriously affect those around you, it also has a profound affect on you as well.

It can chip away at all the good in your life until it is almost non-existent. Unresolved emotional issues can harden your heart, making you cold and totally void of any compassion for others. Your bitterness for some can cause you to lose the ability to empathize or sympathize with others. Past hurtful feelings can also cause you physical and emotional pain. Lastly, your spiritual relationship with God can begin to deteriorate as you cling to your painful past.

College professor and author Cassandra George Sturges, Psy.D. wrote the following in her book *The Illusion of Beauty: Why Women Hate Themselves and Other Women:*

"As black women, I wonder if sometimes we are too bitter when sweetness is in order; too stern when being laid-back would suffice and too hard when softness could do it so much better. Maybe it is impossible for us to give our men, what we are seeking to obtain for ourselves. Maybe it's difficult to trust with shattered faith, love unconditionally with a bruised heart and support someone else's dream with a broken spirit. Because the typical American white woman's past did not contain the same type of pain as the American black woman, her vision of the black man is not blurred with criticisms and expectations."

So how do you break the cycle? How do you heal from past hurt and pain? How do you go from being angry, mean, bitter and spiteful to displaying a pleasant attitude? Well, the first step to overcoming anger is identifying the cause of your anger. Some people struggle with anger for so long that they forget the root cause of their anger. When you identify what you're truly angry about you can begin the process of healing.

Second, you must forgive the person or persons who caused you pain in your life. I know that's a hard pill to swallow but it must be done. True deliverance from the emotional bondage that you're in starts with forgiveness. One of the thorniest and most difficult things we are ever called upon to do is to respond to evil with kindness, and to forgive the unforgivable. Yet study after study shows that one of the keys to longevity and good health is to develop a habit of gratitude and let go of past hurts.

Your offender may not deserve to be forgiven for all the pain and sadness and suffering purposefully inflicted on your life, but *you* deserve to be free. Forgiveness gives you a kind of freedom that makes it well worth letting go of what happened in your past. It takes more energy to hate a person then it does to forgive and let go so you can move on with your life. Whether it was molestation, abuse, infidelity, betrayal, deceit or any other harmful behavior, forgiveness will take you one step closer to having a positive attitude and disposition in life.

Third, forgive yourself. Often times women have a problem forgiving themselves for the decisions of their past. They hold themselves hostage, believing that they are no longer worthy of all the good that life has to offer.

Fourth, pray for them. I know this sounds crazy but I assure you it is not. Even the Bible says pray for them which despitefully use you. Pray for their general well being. This is important because it serves as a true test that you really have forgiven the person. Often, we want harm and retribution to come on those who have hurt us. As long as you seek harm to come on others, you really haven't forgiven them. Ephesians 4:31-32 says, "Get rid of all bitterness, rage and anger, brawling and slander, along with every form of malice. Be kind and compassionate to one another, forgiving each other, just as in Christ God forgave you."

When you pray, pray in this manner:

Father, I acknowledge that I've held resentment and bitterness against _____. I confess this as sin and ask you to forgive me. I forgive _____. Remind me, Lord, to not hold any more resentment, but rather to love this person. Father, I ask you to also forgive _____.

Thank you for hearing and answering my prayer. In Jesus' name, Amen.

How liberating it will be when you pray for all of those who have spitefully used you.

Lastly, enjoy your life. Take the time to smell the flowers. Look for the good in people. Celebrate your accomplishments. Be genuinely happy for others. Walk around with a smile on your face. Don't take life so seriously. Have a sense of humor about things. Laugh as often as you can. When difficult times and difficult people come your way, know that it is just a test that you must pass in order to continue to move forward in your life.

Black Women Who Hate On Other Women

I'm sure that most of you are familiar with the biblical story of Cain and Abel. If you are not, let me quickly bring you up to speed. The story of Cain and Abel appears in the first 16 verses of the fourth chapter in the Book of Genesis.

Cain and Abel were the sons of Adam and Eve. Cain, a farmer, and Abel, a shepherd, both made sacrifices of the fruit of their labor to God. God looked favorably upon Abel's sacrifice, but not Cain's. In his anger over the incident, Cain murdered his brother.

God asked Cain where his brother was, and Cain replied, "I don't know. Am I my brother's keeper?" God knew that Cain had killed Abel and ultimately punished him by making him a "restless wanderer." With his question, "Am I my brother's keeper?" Cain attempted to throw the scent off his misdeed by claiming no responsibility regarding his brother.

Followers of biblical teachings often interpret this story as a reminder that they are responsible for the welfare of others. So, my brother's keeper has come to refer to a person who looks out for and cares for others, whether literally brothers or sisters or not. There should be no difference concerning women.

As Black women it's time to lift each other up every chance you get. It's time to honor your sisterhood and cheer the talents you each bring to the table. It's time to make a pact to support one another. You should reach across the obstacles of age, physical features, jobs, financial status, and social class to embrace each other.

When you can walk into a room and feel good about yourself, you won't feel the need to tear the next woman down. So what if she's got a bald spot in the back of her head. That's her bald spot. Who cares if her outfit doesn't measure up to your standard of acceptability? That's her personal fashion statement. Stop judging her body. I'm quite sure you have your own physical imperfections.

It's time out for all of that. There are too many other important issues in the world to worry about. Stop hatin', judgin' and gossipin' about your fellow sistahs. Just let it go. Instead, self-reflect. Take a long look at yourself and deal with your own issues. Overcome your own insecurities. We ALL have them. Learn to get comfortable in your own skin. Learn to truly love yourself. Intrinsic to true sisterhood is self-love, self esteem, and understanding and accepting who you are.

Stop looking at other women as the enemy. Stop trying to emulate TV reality-star NeNe from *The* Real Housewives of Atlanta. Her backbiting, confrontational and drama creating antics should not be admired but abhorred. VH-1's urban queen 'New York' aka Tiffany Pollard should not be idolized but challenged for her less than admirable qualities. Rather than tuning in for the next big dramatic scene to tantalize your senses, keep in mind that reality TV is far from real. They are not as outrageous as they portray themselves to be.

Do I know these women personally? No. However, as a television personality myself, I know how the media seeks to create scenarios to bring out the outrageous in order to increase and maintain its viewing audience. The media machine has done a great job perpetuating the notion that Black women are the enemy of one another and just can't get along. Just watch an episode of reality TV shows *The Flavor of Love*, *For The Love of Ray J* or *Charm School*. The combination of scripted drama scenes, lots of alcohol and cameras rolling is enough to convince the world that Black women just can't get along.

Black women can absolutely get along. But in order to do that it's important to learn one very important thing. So, Black women, please take heed to these instructions of love. Stop hatin' on one another.

Mothers stop hatin' on your daughters because they were able to accomplish things in life that you could not. Pursue your dreams, it's not too late. Daughters stop hatin' on your mothers for not living the life you think they should live. They may not have had all the opportunities that you have been exposed to. Sisters stop hatin' on your siblings because you may have always lived in their shadow. Be your own person. Women stop hatin' on your girlfriends because they have a man and you don't or because they've got a good man and yours is triflin'. Make better choices.

Stop hatin' on your co-worker because you don't believe she deserved the raise or promotion she got. Work harder. Stop hatin' on another woman's shape, or complexion or length of hair. Learn to love your own attributes and work with them. With regard to features that are out of your control, heed the words of that famous prayer: "Lord grant me the serenity to accept the things I cannot change, the courage to change the things I can, and the wisdom to know the difference."

Instead, learn to love yourself and love your neighbor (fellow sistah) as you would yourself. Learn to appreciate your differences and make them strengths that bind you all together. Learn to celebrate each other's accomplishments. Rather than trying to pull each other down like crabs in a barrel, learn to allow others to pull you up. Learn to be genuinely happy for others despite your personal hardships.

Nearly all women can attest to having had something happen in their life that has left them bitter or negative for, at least, a small period of time. But don't take your personal pain out on others. Rather, allow the goodness in others to bring out the healing in you. Once that practice is successfully established, we all can move from hatin' on Black women to lovin' on Black women.

Why Black Men Don't Want You

A growing number of African American men are leaving Black women for the alternative other: White, Latin, and Asian women. Up until 1967, U.S law prohibited marriage outside of one's race. Once the law was reversed people amongst a multitude of ethnicities began to inter-marry and the numbers of reported unions have gone up each year.

To give you an idea of the marriage statistics when it comes to interracial marriage, the 2008 U.S census report revealed some very interesting statistics which can be found on http://www.blackstate.com/interracialdating909.html. The numbers tell a very interesting story.

- Black husbands: Married 310,000 White women - Married 4,190,000 Black women Married 39,700 Asian women.
- White husbands: Married 55,399,200 White women - Married 137,000 Black women - Married 713,000 Asian women.
- Asian husbands: Married 193,000 White women - Married 8,400 Black women - Married 2,790,000 Asian women.

Two glaring facts stand out based upon the reported data. First, Black men lead the pack in interracial marriage by a significant margin in comparison to their White and Asian counterpart. Second, Black men are marrying far more Black women than White women. So, even though they outnumber men of other races, the interracial-marriage statistics for Black men are quite small.

What these numbers don't account for is the number of Black men who date and/or sex outside of their race but choose to marry Black.

Nevertheless, these numbers should encourage Black women who are seeking marriage. Our community has been sold a false idea that an overwhelming number of Black men have abandoned ship. Though, a significant number of men have, more have apparently not gone anywhere. Keep in mind, the chapter 'Why Black Men Don't Want You' shares a survey that I discovered titled *The Top Ten Reasons Why It's Hard To Date A Black Woman* by Matthew Lynch.

The article indicates that Black men do date and marry Black women. However, the survey expresses their personal feelings regarding how difficult it can be to date and/or marry a Black woman. What must be stated is that scores of Black men have been complaining about many of these issues for years. In fact, the same general complaints are discussed over and over and over again. So, there must be some validity to it. They all can't be crazy. There must be threads of truth somewhere.

So here's my advice. First, accept the fact that some men are just gonna date outside of their race. It's going to continue to happen whether you like it or not. It's just a fact of life. So, if you are one of those sistahs who get an attitude every time you see a Black man with White, Latina, or Asian women get over it. No matter how you feel about it you won't be able to change it. Just let go and let God.

Second, take the time to pause, re-read and ponder on what has been written in the aforementioned chapter. It's very easy to become offended by the statements. Especially when you feel like you've been attacked. But I encourage you to self reflect. Most women who I've personally interviewed initially became very offended upon reading or hearing why some Black men don't want Black women. However, after further consideration many admitted to the validity of the list.

Take a self-assessment test. Honestly ask yourself if you reflect any of the items mentioned on the list. After you have completed that, share the list within your spheres of influence. Go to people who have your best interest at heart and are willing to be honest and transparent with you. That could possibly be a parent, grandparent, sibling, friend, mentor, co-worker, spouse, love interest or even a former love interest.

Review the list with them and get their honest feedback. Sometimes people can observe things in us that we aren't aware of ourselves. If you reflect any characteristic or behavior on the list you can apply the next step. Third, commit to a season of personal growth and self development. We all have habits, shortcomings and idiosyncrasies that can be worked on in our lives. Not only will the change make for a better person, but for a better relationship as well.

Consider the following statement written by college professor and author Cassandra George Sturges Psy.D. in her book *The Illusion of Beauty: Why Women Hate Themselves and other Women:*

I think it's less painful for us as black women to believe that black men desire white women because her hair blows in the wind and her eyes are sparkling blue. We want to believe this because we don't have to look within our own souls for answers that may be painful. We would then have to question our role as "superwoman" and self-righteous, martyrs. We don't want to believe that maybe it's not the stereotypes that we hear about white women being docile and sexually uninhibited. We chant to ourselves how we pay the bills, wash his clothes and cook his dinner, but when he steps out of line we are there with a tongue-lashing to make sure that he recognizes and appreciates our hard work.

The commitment to personal growth and self development in no way implies that if you as a woman get yourself together you'll finally get a man. That would also imply that women are the problem. Some of men's complaints about Black women may be due in part to their warped socialization process regarding women and their roles, responsibilities and behavior. So both men and women share in the responsibility of healing themselves. When that is successfully done their relationships will heal.

Can A Sistah Get Some Love?

Write Your List Then Become It. In order to secure a good Black man, it's important to know what a good Black man is. Interestingly, if you were to ask ten different women to provide a definition you would most likely receive ten different responses. Why? It's simple. The answer is based upon a woman's age, maturity level, experience, interests, passions, personal needs, desires and expectations.

So, in your quest to find a good man, it's important to properly assess yourself first and then make wise choices based upon that assessment. For a thorough analysis that will help you find a good man go to www.whywehateblackwomen.com and take Hasani's Relationship Questionnaire. It is a comprehensive questionnaire that will help you clarify what you're looking for in a potential date/mate. It will also cover dating non-negotiables and deal breakers.

After completing the questionnaire you will soon discover that a good man is not going to meet every item on your checklist, nor should he. If he did, that would make him ideal (perfect). Once you've created your list and know what it is you're looking for, become the person you seek. Do pursue what you don't represent yourself. The law of attraction states that you draw to yourself who and what you are. So, if you know you have issues, get yourself together first and then hold him up to a similar standard.

Date A Man Like An Employer. If you treat the dating season like a job then it's nothing more than a selection process. In other words, it's a process of elimination. When an employer seeks to hire someone for a particular position, the company goes through an intensive selection process. If you are the applicant, the company requires that you make a case in support of your potential employment.

You must present a resume with your work experience, educational background, skill sets and personal accomplishments. At the top of the resume you must indicate your objective for applying for the position. Your resume, as an initial representation of you, will be assessed to determine whether or not you're a match for the company.

You must then fill out their application, which asks you to provide personal and professional references that can vouch for you. You must also provide verifiable information about your previous employers and the role you played with them. You must then go through an intense interview process with members of the company who will assess you from different perspectives. They will collectively make a unanimous decision whether or not to hire you.

If you are selected, you must then go through a number of tests and checks: drug tests, blood tests, criminal background checks, credit checks, etc. A lot goes into hiring someone for a position within a company. Psychologist Jawanza Kunjufu said, "We do a better job of choosing our cars, clothes, colleges and careers than we do selecting a mate." If we were half as careful selecting a partner, as a company is selecting an employee, our relationships would be in much better shape.

Play Detective But Act Naïve. Going back to the employment example, once you get hired you get placed on a 90 Day probationary period. During that time the company wants to assess your performance, test your skills and determine whether you're a good fit for the company. They state upfront that you have 90 days to prove yourself.

They observe your work performance, monitor your communication (email/phone) and conduct evaluations on you. Should dating be any different? Whenever you enter into a relationship you should take the time to get to know as much as you can about a person. Why? Because just like a job people know how to fudge a resume and lie their way through an interview. So, you have to investigate in order to determine whether the person lives up to everything that they initially displayed.

Remember, you don't really know this joker. He could be crazy. So many women have been lied to, taken advantage of, robbed, raped and ridiculed because they really didn't take the time to play detective while acting naïve. Get to know his friends and family. Observe him around others. Pay attention to his conversations. People tell a lot about themselves if you just listen. Observe his habits. See where he lives. Does he live with his mother or is he on his own? Does he really have a job or is he hustling on the side? Ask around and find out about his reputation. Put all the pieces of the puzzle together and see how the picture turns out.

Keep Your Legs Closed. Don't be so free with your body. Men can have sex without commitment fairly easily. They can certainly have it without love. For many men, sex and a relationship do not necessarily have anything to do with each other. If you want to keep your value and worth with a man make him work for your affection. Men like to hunt. They like a challenge. Don't be his 'easy in, easy out'. He won't respect you. In fact, he typically will categorize you and put you in his freak box.

You see, a lot of men have a friend box, a freak box and a girlfriend/potential partner box. You have the power to control which box you allow a man to put you in. If a man truly wants you, he will adjust to your plan and wait. I know I did. One year and a half later, I was married.

Embrace Your Season. In life we have four seasons: spring, summer, fall and winter. They are all unique and different. You must learn how to properly adjust to each season of life in order be successful. Likewise, in relationships there are four seasons: dating, committed courtship, engagement and marriage. They also come with their own set of rules, responsibilities, levels of commitment, and expectations. If you truly want to be in a healthy relationship you must learn how to successfully function in each season in order to graduate into the next season.

Read books, go to seminars, join organizations like 'Black Women Who Want More,' participate in social networks, find healthy couples to model, and be willing to CHANGE. If you treat life like one big classroom you will be surprised what wonders it will do for you and your relationship.

Numerous books, short films, documentaries, seminars and talk shows have been dedicated to discussing the problems that Black men and Black women face within their relationships as well as within society. Scholars, experts, media personalities and the general public have all weighed in and contributed to the discussion. Unfortunately, in many respects, a discussion is all that it has ever amounted to. We typically have very spirited meetings, where we discuss many great ideas, but then we go back to business as usual.

Don't let another opportunity for change pass by. Now is the time. It's time to take back your lives. It's time to be the best you that you can be. It's time to celebrate the best of who you are. Use this book as a tool for education, enlightenment and empowerment. After you have read it, pass it along and let it make a difference in someone else's life. Finally, make the decision to take part in letting the world know "Why We Hate Black Women" and "Why We Should Love Them."

Black Women Who Want More

Hell knows no fury like a Black woman scorned.
~Anonymous

*I*n the early stages of this writing endeavor I flew out to Atlanta for a television interview with TV-One's Black Men Revealed. Once the show aired I received many calls and emails about my appearance. One of the calls was from a woman who belonged to an organization called Black Women Who Want More. I was immediately intrigued by this all-Black women's Philadelphia-based organization.

After meeting with its founding members I immediately had them on my radio show. Their wisdom, poise, and vision for Black women overwhelmingly impressed me. I was then invited to attend a number of their meet-ups in the local area. I met Black women of all ages, faiths, relational statuses, and socio-economic backgrounds who all united around one common mission. In the words of president and founder Renee Toppin:

"Black Women Who Want More are an organization of Black women who are striving to be spiritually grounded, emotionally stable, physically fit, financially poised, intellectually enlightened, politically conscious and socially gracious. We are women who want more, demand more and deserve more of the best that life has to offer. We are on a journey to become our best selves. As broken vessels, we must first consult the master builder, the potter who carefully crafted us and made us the beautiful creatures that we are. Spiritual wholeness is the first step in the journey. We must learn the art of submission; we must regain trust in God and re-assert our trust in our Black men.

Once we are spiritually whole, the rest of the pieces will come together as our ordered steps take us forward in this journey. As we love ourselves MORE, others will love us MORE. As we respect ourselves MORE, others will respect us MORE. The hate will dissipate as we are seen in the light of our wholeness. We will be complete, no longer looking for someone else to complete us or to fill the empty spaces in our hearts, our bodies, our finances or our souls. This is the end of that journey, and the beginning of MORE."

Not only do the women in this organization demand more of themselves, they desire more in Black men as well. And what they are asking for reflects what countless Black women across the country are asking for. They want more love, more compassion, more respect, more support, more acknowledgment, more relationships, more, truthfulness, more spirituality, more leadership, more commitment, more solidarity and more faithfulness. Not only do Black women want more, they deserve more.

As Black men, many of us have been excellent examples of men, fathers and husbands. We've been providers, protectors, mentors and true friends to our women. We've fought for them not with them. We've been their strength in moments of weakness and vulnerability. We've been the fulfillment of many of their hopes and dreams.

With that said, we've also been the biggest source of their pain. We've cheated on them, abused them, lied to them, betrayed them, abandoned them, and devalued them. We've been irresponsible, undependable, unsupportive, and emotionally and physically unavailable.

Black women want two simple things from Black men. They want the first group of men to <u>do more</u> of what they're already doing. However, they want the second group of men to <u>be more</u> than what they presently are. If we both, as Black men and women, begin to reflect on our personal thoughts, deed, and actions and take the time to commit to a lifestyle of CANI (constant and never-ending improvement), our relationships will begin to heal.

As I travel the country I am often confronted with a question that many Black men desire to know the answer to: "What do women really want from us?" So, I decided to ask them.

Good evening. My perspective is from a 34 year-old single Black woman no kids. The number one thing I want from a Black man is a shared belief and lifestyle grounded in Jesus. I feel strongly with a foundation in Christ all other issues can be overcome. The Word will be our blueprint in how to come together, how to treat each other within the union and how to stay together.

Kishonda

What I want in a Black man is integrity, compassion, honesty, ambition, love and sincere companionship. Integrity meaning being the man and upholding the morals that God set forth not a man whose image is based upon what society says you're supposed to be. A man who is true to his word, who is the provider, who is faithful, who treats his woman as his equal not as someone who is beneath him. Compassion means continuing to show the passion, affection, and love that you showed in the beginning of the relationship when you were trying to earn that woman. I want a man who knows how to keep the fire burning and the relationship exciting.

Janeen

Honesty and communication is key. Men tend to be very vocal when something is bothering them but clam up when it comes to exposing their feelings for a woman. And women often feel if you cannot verbalize your love for us then you and her are on two different pages. A man needs to be honest on all levels even if he feels she may not like what he is really thinking. It still needs to be brought to the table so we can address the issue. Especially if it's something that can harm the relationship, it needs to be discussed so it can be resolved. I know a lot of times men don't want to hear women's reactions due to the dramatics and emotions, but the man's delivery controls our reaction so communicate carefully.

Amanda

We want quality time. This is time when your focus is on her exclusively. Not sitting in the same room while you watch the game or check your email. It's time when you just put work and the rest of the world on hold and give her your complete attention (no phone, no email no interruptions). We want those massages without asking for it, we still want flowers sent to our job just because you were thinking about us, we still want the surprise gifts, we still want dinner dates and we still want the simple walks, watching the sunset together or cuddling up watching a movie. This is quality time that doesn't cost a dime.

Ashley

As a Black woman, I want honesty, communication, support, and respect. I need a Black man to stand by me, lift me up, be there for me when I'm down, to laugh and cry with me. In the last couple of years, Black men have let me down. They have fallen short on what they're supposed to do and be. I pray that they realize how they have been treating their Black women (wives, girlfriends, mothers, children and sister-friends) and begin doing right by them. We are not bitches. We are not whores. We are not sluts. We are Women. We are Ladies. We are Diamonds.

Damaris

As a Black woman I want a man to be a MAN. I want to feel protected by him, loved by him, be treated as his equal his partner for life, and the love of his life. I want understanding and communication. I want him to open up his heart and listen not just with his ears but with his heart. I want him to feel what I feel and get a better understanding of what I'm going through.

If I came home from work I want him to ask how my day was instead of having to tell him to ask me. I want him to pray with and for me. I want him to be the head of the home. I want a hard working man, not a video game playing man. I want someone who can form a complete sentence and know how to order from the right side of menu when we eat out. He needs to know that filet mignon is steak not fish.

LaToya

Having had to live with the fact that 1) my father abandoned our family, 2) I've had two failed marriages and still desire the companionship of a good Black man and 3) I have two sons (who will someday be husbands) and one daughter (who will someday have a husband); the only thing that I would require out of a Black man today is honesty. Honesty covers the gamut.

Why We Hate Black Women

If a Black man is honest then he won't lie about himself - past, present or future. If a Black man is honest, he is capable of partaking in an open discussion. If a Black man is honest a couple's progress and growth would be infinite. If a Black man is honest, then his woman wouldn't have to worry about infidelity. And, even if he did cheat, the drama of deception wouldn't be present and it would make it so much easier to forgive and forget- particularly because she knows that her man is honest and what he speaks is the truth!!

If Black men were honest, women would truly know their needs, wants and desires which would compel us to be even greater women to them. If a Black man were honest women wouldn't hate on other women so much because they trust and respect their man- which eliminates a great majority of woman to woman competition, jealousy and hatred. If Black men were honest, Black women wouldn't run around trying to perpetrate, front and pretend to be the woman that they are not. They'd focus on what he wants, because they know it is truly the area in which their attention is required.

Finally, if Black men were honest, it would force women to be more honest with themselves, and their man. It would break down walls; years and years of perpetual self-hatred, blaming of others, immaturity and low self-esteem. Can you imagine the healing that would take place, if Black men were just honest?

Ge'ylah

Fidelity - This goes without saying. If you are with me, then be only with me. If you feel that you are lacking something in the relationship, let me know first so that we can work on it. I firmly believe that what you won't do another woman will. With that being said, give me the opportunity to do what needs to be done and make whatever necessary changes that need to take place in order for our relationship to thrive. Don't just go looking for it somewhere else.

Emotionally Accessible - Black men have a tendency to hide their emotions. This creates a barrier. We need men to let us know how they are feeling, to allow themselves to be vulnerable. If you can't be vulnerable with your significant other, than who can you be vulnerable with? And we women should not use their ability to get emotional against them. If a man cries in front of us, then don't throw it back in his face later down the line when you get in an argument. On the same note, men can't judge a book by "another woman's cover." Don't assume your present woman is going to be like your last. An ex is an ex for a reason, so I highly doubt that you are going to go to a woman who's just like the one you just left.   Quamara

As a Black woman, I would like Black men to think about their actions/ reactions towards women of color. I understand that society has accepted more diverse relationships, however, women of color are being judged by perceptions that we have attitude and are quick to argue our positions.... I would like to see Black men become more honest with themselves and their internal struggles... If you need a psychologist to work out your deep seated problems then there is nothing wrong with reaching out for one.

I would like Black men to make an effort to get to know who they are dealing with versus anticipating a sexual conquest and having women believe you are interested, knowing that your intentions are contrary to your actions. Black men tend to become complacent in their outlook on dating.... There are many things that can be explored that are free or have a nominal charge...

Men know whether or not a relationship is worth investing time ...If you are just coming out of a long term relationship, divorce, or

217

living with someone tell her that... if you are having a sexual relationship with someone else ... tell her that.... This gives her the option to think about the values that an honest man would want reciprocated in their woman of choice.... Too many relationships have no boundaries and Black men and women are hurting each other then blaming when they started on dishonesty. But, then Black men choose other mates (cultures) and then profess that it is Black women who are the problem when they have not put forth the effort to make situations better with us.

Rasheeda

In any relationship you must have communication, trust, honesty and the willingness to compromise. I expect a man to be a man of his word to practice and live out what he preaches. Be a man of commitment, integrity and compassion. Men need to know that it's alright to be emotional, compassionate, and cry when there's a need to. I want a man that knows how to love and isn't afraid to show it to the world. I want a man that will take care of me and show me that I don't have to want for nothing.

I want a man that will be intimate with me even when we're not in the bedroom. I want a man that can show he loves me without it being sexual. Men need to show their women that yes they love making love to them but they do things to build up to the moment and not just expect it and nothing has been deposited all day, all week, or all month. It's not enough to hear the sweet nothings while making love but when the love making is over you don't hear the sweet talk.

Things need to be consistent. Marriage is awesome but we have to be willing to work together to make it last and keep things spicy. Sex can really be over rated if the parties involved is not working together to see what pleases each other. Most women can live without sex but to keep their mates happy they give in and do it knowing that they're really not happy. Men you really have to make sure you are taking care of you and yours because what you don't treasure another man will. Not saying that's the right thing but it happens all the time. If your wife or girlfriend isn't hearing what they want to hear from you and another man is telling them what they want to hear, your relationship is headed for disaster.

Toya

I want to feel protected and needed. I don't want to feel like I could be stood up at any moment, or like I am one of a million and my spot can be easily and frequently filled whether I mess up or not. I want a SAVED (not just a dude that goes to church every now and then and prays before most meals) to treat me like a lady. That includes but is not limited to the following: Hold my hand just about everywhere we go, walk on the outside of the street, PAY, give me your jacket when it's cold, stand when I enter a room, introduce me to your mother and sisters as your lady, aspire to be a husband (my husband), aspire to continually go higher and always think of "us" whenever you plan anything, be happy, love hard, be thoughtful-even if being thoughtful is asking your mother or my friends what they think I might like as a date, or a gift or a trip.

Indigo

Black women across the nation are speaking up and speaking out about their love for Black men and their desire for More; more for themselves and more from the men in their lives. If you are a Black woman who wants more in every area of your life, I highly encourage you to go to the back of this book and discover more about the organization *Black Women Who Want More*.

Regardless of your age, occupation, relational status or religious affiliation, there is a place for you within the organization. This Philadelphia-based organization has gone national and chapters are starting all over the country. If you don't have a group in your area, then start one. Likewise, if you are a Black man who wants more then join the brother organization *Black Men Who Want More*.

Whether we all join these organizations or not, living by the principles and creeds of these organizations will 1) celebrate the cultural legacy of Black women in America, 2) strengthen the unity of sisterhood amongst Black women, and 3) challenge Black men and women to take an introspective look at themselves in order to close the ever-increasing historic wedge in Black relationships in order to rebuild our families and our communities. Whatever decision you make, decide to become More.

Notes

Appendix

BLACK THIGHS, BLACK GUYS & BEDROOM LIES is one of the most profound books ever written on relationship which clearly exposes how lust, deception and sexual self-gratification ultimately destroy both the individual and the relationship.

THIS BOOK WILL EXPLAIN:

•In the end every playa gets played
•Sex on campus: the naked truth about the real sex lives of college students
•Can black love survive in America?
•5 things to expect from the bedroom of ecstasy
•The benefits of choosing abstinence over promiscuity

ISBN 0-9707915-1-8 PAPER-BACK - 192 U.S. $14.95

PIMPIN' FROM THE PULPIT TO THE PEWS is an explosive, eye-opening book that reveals how the spirit of lust has crept into the church and has devastatingly affected both its leadership and laity. The book not only exposes the spirit of lust, but offers a step-by-step plan for overcoming sexual sin in order to pursue sexual purity.

THIS BOOK REVEALS:

•How Baal worship has entered into the church
•How inappropriate sexual behavior compromises the integrity of church leadership
•How Satan's fivefold ministry creates an insatiable appetite for sex
•True deliverance for homosexuals within the church
•How to pursue sexual purity after falling into the traps of sexual sin

ISBN 0-9707915-1-8
PAPERBACK - 236 U.S. $14.95

Given the right habits, nearly anyone can succeed in life. In **THE 12 HABITS SERIES** you learn ideas, concepts, and methods used by high-achieving people in almost every field. The book will explore how to unlock your individual potential for personal greatness:

•The 12 Habits of Successful People Explores:
•How Successful People Dream Big Dreams
•How Successful People Aren't Afraid of Failure
•How Successful People Master The Art of Focus
•How Succesful People Are Persistent

ISBN - 0-9707915-3-4 PAPER-BACK - 128 U.S. $7.95
ISBN - 0-9707915-4-2 PAPER-BACK - 126 U.S. $14.95

Black Women Who Want More

Join One Of Our Existing Nationwide Chapters Or Start A Chapter Today!

Join us on our journey to our BEST SELF. This is not just a meetup, this is a MOVEMENT. A movement towards a new generation of Whole Black women who are EMPOWERED in every area of their lives. We refer to ourselves as Diamonds because we are priceless! We bring out the BEST in each other! We plan events that cater to EVERY aspect of our lives. Black Women Who Want More will strengthen your finances, your relationships, your health and emotional well-being and your spirit. We don't plan events, we create experiences. This is the group that you've been waiting for.

To find out more about our organization call us today at 215-307-7070 or visit us at http://www.meetup.com/blackwomenwhowantmore/

My Relationship Is In Trouble: Now What?

PRODUCT ORDER FORM

Send books to:_____

Name:_____

Address:_____

City:_____ State:_____ Zip Code:_____

Phone:_____

Email:_____

OPTIONAL:

Credit Card Info:

Card Type: ☐ Visa ☐ Master Card ☐ Discover ☐ AMEX

CC #:_____

Exp. Date:_____/_____/_____

3 digit #:_____

Signature:_____

PRODUCTS BEING ORDERED ARE AS FOLLOWS:

Book Titles Quantity Unit Price Total	PRICE	QTY
Why We Hate Black Women	$16.95	_____
Pimpin' From The Pulpit To The Pews	$14.95	_____
Black Thighs, Black Guys & Bedroom Lies	$14.95	_____
The 12 Habits of Successful People	$7.95	_____
The 12 Habits of Healthy People	$7.95	_____
CD TITLES		
Abortion: A Woman's Right or WRONG!	$14.95	_____
Christians Get STDs Too! (mp3 available)	$14.95	_____
Generation XXX (mp3 available)	$14.95	_____
Subtotal for all items	_____	_____
Add Postage (1-5 items $6.50 / 6-15 items $11.50)	_____	_____
Total for Order	_____	_____

THERE ARE THREE WAYS TO ORDER PRODUCTS FROM Hasani Pettiford Enterprises:

1 CALL toll free at **888-237-6101** and place your order over the phone.

2 FAX this order form to **888-237-6101** toll free phone / fax (Credit Card only).

3 MAIL this order form with money order to: Hasani Pettiford Enterprises, PO Box 24 Williamstown, NJ 08094